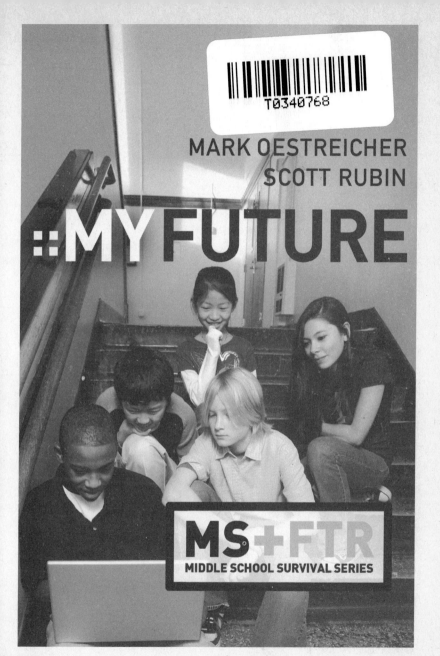

MARK OESTREICHER
SCOTT RUBIN

::MY FUTURE

MS+FTR
MIDDLE SCHOOL SURVIVAL SERIES

ZONDERVAN®

ZONDERVAN.com/
AUTHORTRACKER
follow your favorite authors

invert

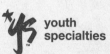youth
specialties

08 09 10 11 12 • 20 19 18 17 16 15 14 13 12 11 10 9 8 7 6 5 4 3 2 1

DEDICATION

This book is dedicated to our sons—all future middle schoolers!—Max Oestreicher, and Tanner, Dawson, and Brock Rubin. What a crazy-cool privilege it is to see you rocketing into your own exciting futures!

ACKNOWLEDGMENTS

Scott wants to thank Lynette, Tanner, Dawson, and Brock—
"Team Rubin." You're my four favorite people on the planet.
Thanks also to my Elevate teammates: Jason, Brandon, Wes,
Courtney, Phil, Leah, Chris, and Melissa. How do we have this
much fun while *pointing out Jesus* to junior highers scat-
tered around Chicagoland? I also want to thank my friends at
Regular Joe's Coffeehouse for providing a tremendous place to
write, think, and drink. And thanks to God, for loving me.

Marko wants to thank his shockingly amazing family: Jeannie,
Liesl, and Max. I sure do love you guys. Big thanks to my YS
peeps, also—you make my work fun. I didn't write this book at
a coffee shop like I normally do, so I guess I should thank my
backyard and the patio at YS!

■■ CONTENTS

SECTION 11: MARRIAGE

SECTION 12: RIGHTS AND PRIVILEGES (BARELY LEGAL)

SECTION 13: DEATH

SECTION 14: FOR YOUR GENERATION

SECTION 15: IMAGINE

A FINAL THOUGHT

INTRODUCTION

See this really dorky picture right here? That's me, Marko, when I was in middle school. Nice shirt collar, huh? Can you tell I wasn't the most popular kid in school? Uh, yeah.

How about this groovy picture? That's me, Scott, back during my middle school years. That haircut *rocked*, huh? Sure, whatever.

We wanted you to see those pictures—as embarrassing as they are—because we want you to know that we remember what it's like to be a middle school student. Partly we remember because we've been working with middle schoolers in churches for a long time. We don't work with high school kids or with any other age group. That's because we're both convinced of a few things:

- First, middle schoolers are the coolest people in the world. Really! We'd rather hang out with a group of middle school students than any other age group.

- Next, God really cares (we mean, *REALLY CARES*) about middle school students—about you. And we believe God is stoked about the possibility of having a close relationship with you.

- Finally, the middle school years (from about 11 to 14 years old) are HUGELY important in building a FAITH that will last for your whole life.

This book is the sixth and final book of the Middle School Survival Series. The first book is all about your faith (that's why it's called *My Faith*—duh!). The second book is about your family (it's called, not-so-surprisingly, *My Family*). The third book is about you and your friends (it's called *My Friends*). The fourth book is all about school—it's called *My School*. And the fifth book is about the massive changes you go through during middle school, so we named it *My Changes*. (We're so smart!) We hope you'll read them all!

Oh, one more thing: You don't have to read these 75 "chapters" in any particular order. It's not that kind of book. You can read them in order if you want (if you're one of those people who likes order); or you *can* just flip through and read whatever catches your attention.

We believe in you, and we'll be praying for you (really, we will) that while you read this, you'll grow in your understanding of God (just like the Bible says Jesus did when he was your age), of how much God loves you, and of how God would do anything to let you know him.

Marko and Scott

SECTION 1

MY FUTURE

1. WHY WE WROTE THIS BOOK FOR YOU

Do you ever think much about your past? The past includes all of your little-kid years, but it also includes last week. Basically, the past is whatever stuff is in your memory.

Or maybe you're a person who likes to focus on the present—this moment right now when you're reading these words.

But how much thought do you give to the future? Hmm...?

What's past is already gone. There's no changing that around. But the FUTURE is full of possibilities.

WHAT IF...?   I WONDER...?   COULD I...?

Some of it seems amazing and exciting. Some of it can feel uncertain and even worrisome. And *you* get to choose!

When you were younger, you probably didn't think about the future much. You woke up in the morning, played with some toys, cried 'til someone gave you some food, watched some *Jimmy Neutron*, then played some more—you get the picture. "The future" didn't mean much to you. You didn't really care what day or time it was, and you certainly didn't think about what would happen that day—you just took things as they came.

But now—in your middle school years—the future is taking on a whole new meaning. And even though it can feel scary sometimes—it can also be thrilling, especially if you're ready for it.

We (Marko and Scott) love helping middle school students think about—and get ready for—their futures. Some people look at middle schoolers and think, *Those punks have so much growing up to do. Why bother talking to them about the future now?* But we know there are lots of things bouncing around in middle schoolers' brains. Some of them are about the "near future"—things you'll experience in the next few years (or even weeks and months). Some are about things in the "way-out-there future"—things you won't have to deal with for many years. But the thoughts you're having *now* will direct your future.

What you've just read is already in the past, so let's dive right into (drum roll, please) *your future!*

2. WHAT THE BIBLE SAYS ABOUT THE FUTURE

Let's start with a handful of Bible verses about the future:

> When times are good, be happy; but when times are bad, consider: God has made the one as well as the other. Therefore, you cannot discover anything about your future. (Ecclesiastes 7:14)

> Since no one knows the future, who can say what is to come? (Ecclesiastes 8:7)

> "For I know the plans I have for you," declares the Lord, "plans to prosper you and not to harm you, plans to give you hope and a future." (Jeremiah 29:11)

> Can any one of you by worrying add a single hour to your life? (Matthew 6:27)

> For I am convinced that neither death nor life, neither angels nor demons, neither the present nor the future, nor any powers, neither height nor depth, nor anything else in all creation, will be able to separate us from the love of God that is in Christ Jesus our Lord. (Romans 8:38-39)

Wow! We can learn some fantastic things in those verses right there, stuff about how we should approach thinking about the future. These Scriptures are pretty much saying, "Don't worry about the future: God has great plans for you, and God will be with you. The future can't separate you from God!"

Seriously, that's some good stuff. Maybe you don't need to read the rest of this book.

DECISIONS

3. PROS AND CONS

We hear lots of parents say stuff to their little kids like, "Make wise choices, honey." That's just a gentle reminder for younger kids to think before they do something. It's like saying, "Remember to look both ways before you cross the street," or "Remember not to eat yellow snow," or "Please don't duct-tape your little sister to the wall."

But as you get older, decisions get more complicated, don't they? Choosing wisely is still...well, wise. But the stuff you're deciding isn't as plain and simple as it used to be. If you say yes to some things, then both good *and* bad stuff can happen—from the very same decision.

Maybe you've heard of "pros and cons." It's a shorter way of saying "arguments *for* and arguments *against*." When you're making big decisions, it can be helpful to write a list of the pros and cons so you can see the possible outcomes of your choice. Thinking about decisions in this way really can help you choose the best option.

Let's try an example. Suppose your friends are hanging out at your house, and you're all bored. One of your friends says he heard that cats always land on their feet, even if they're dropped from a high place. Then he says, "Let's throw your little sister's cat off the roof of the school and see if it's true!"

Hmmmm...

PROS

- Your friends will probably laugh, and they might think you're cool or fun.

- You'll know for sure whether sweet little Fluffy really does always land on her feet.

CONS

- Your parents will probably get mad and ground you.

- You could easily slip off the roof and end up in the hospital.

- Your little sister will be soooo mad if you throw Fluffy.

- Fluffy could die. Messily.

That's just a short list. You probably wouldn't even need a paper and pencil to figure this out, but the cons outweigh the pros by a factor of two. This information should lead you to realize it's probably a bad decision to throw Fluffy off the roof.

Okay, maybe this example wasn't the most serious of all possible examples. But choosing wisely with a "pros and cons" strategy can be helpful even when you're making the toughest decisions.

4. WHO INFLUENCES MY DECISIONS?

One of the best parts of getting older is that you get to make more decisions *on your own.* Your mom and dad are no longer deciding practically everything for you like they did when you were younger: What you wear, what you eat, where you go, and how long you stay.

Sure, you don't get to make *all* your own decisions yet. But one of the keys to being allowed to make more choices is knowing who influences your decisions. *Influence* is simply "the ability to affect" you.

WHO HAS THE ABILITY TO AFFECT YOU?
There are some obvious ones: Your parents, your friends, and maybe your brother or sister.

CAN PEOPLE WHO *AREN'T* YOUR FRIENDS INFLUENCE YOU?
Absolutely! Even the bully who gives you a hard time at school can influence you and affect your decisions. For instance, if you take a different route to your next class in order to avoid him, then he's influenced you. We *often* let people—even people who aren't our friends—influence the way we act or dress or talk simply because we believe we'll be more popular or accepted. But we can choose whether they affect us.

CAN PEOPLE YOU DON'T EVEN *KNOW* AFFECT YOU?
Without a doubt! For example, advertising companies receive a mountain of cash so they can impact the way you spend *your* money, the way you look at fashion and style, the way you decide what to watch

and listen to and even believe. *Their ultimate goal is to influence you!*

The best news is that *you* **have a choice** about what influences you. But in order to control those influences and not let them take over your brain, you need to know who—specifically—is influencing you. Right now, make a list of adults, kids, companies, shows, and music that influence you and the decisions you make. You can even write your list in the blank space along the side of this page, right over there. When you're done, look it over and decide if you want to change who and what is on that list.

Then YOU can have more control of who YOU become!

5. WHERE DOES GOD FIT?

Because you're really smart (we know it's true cuz you're reading this book), you'd probably guess that we (Marko and Scott) believe God should definitely play a key role in the decisions you make. Wow! You *are* smart!

But now two more questions come to mind: *Why?* and *How?*

WHY SHOULD GOD FIT INTO MY DECISIONS?

Well, it's not because God is like the lifeguard of a cosmic pool, just waiting to catch you running on the deck so he can shout, "Bad decision!" It's because God is the Creator of wisdom and God really wants great things for you.

> Trust in the Lord with all your heart
> and lean not on your own understanding;
> in all your ways submit to him,
> and he will make your paths straight.
>
> (Proverbs 3:5-6)

"He will make your paths straight" means God will help you live wisely. God's guidance will lead you to good things—and away from unnecessary pain.

Maybe you're already convinced of the "why," but it's the "how" you're after. If there were a Web site where you could type in your questions to God and receive responses, you'd be all over it. So...

HOW DO I LET GOD FIT INTO MY DECISIONS?

Proverbs 2:6 says, "For the Lord gives **wisdom**; from his mouth come knowledge and understanding" (emphasis added). But if God doesn't ring your doorbell whenever you have questions, where do you look for this wisdom? Here are two GREAT options:

1. THE BIBLE—WISDOM STRAIGHT FROM GOD

There's nothing better to look at than God's own words. Just by reading the Bible, you'll get a sense of what God values and what God wants *you* to value. Many student Bibles have a topical index that will lead you to sections of Scripture related to the decisions you're making. Using this and other Bible tools will point you to the parts that talk about the stuff you're thinking about: Friends, parents, pressure, popularity, choices, reputation—and many more.

2. WISE JESUS-FOLLOWERS

Sometimes wise Jesus-followers are the best places to seek wisdom. Ask them to show you the places in the Bible where God talks about the issues you're dealing with. And consider asking them how they've dealt with something similar in the past. They'll probably feel honored that you asked.

"I WANT TO HAVE TIME FOR GOD, BUT IT SEEMS LIKE I HAVE NO TIME. IT'S SO FRUSTRATING."
—MELISSA, 7TH GRADE

6. TIMING: WHAT ABOUT WHEN "I DON'T KNOW" IS REALLY THE ONLY ANSWER I HAVE?

"I don't know."

Does that sound like a "right" answer to you? (We bet you wish your teacher thought so.) Sometimes, no matter how much thought you've given to something, "I don't know" is honestly the only answer you can come up with.

When "I don't know" is all you've got, ask yourself these three questions:

1. DO I REALLY *HAVE* TO MAKE THIS DECISION RIGHT NOW?

When you're trying to decide between A and B, sometimes there could be an answer C (which might stand for "Can it wait?"). Maybe you're not sure whether you want to attend Michigan State University or the University of Southern California. A choice of C could mean reminding yourself that middle schoolers don't have to mail in their college applications for a while. But there are other present-day choices that can also wait. And it's likely that after a day, a week, or a month, you'll receive more information that will make your decision much clearer. So...can it wait?

2. IS THERE REALLY ONLY *ONE* RIGHT DECISION?

You know those crazy test questions with answers A, B, C, D, and the dreaded E—*all of the above?* Man, we hated those questions! Or answers like "A,

B, *and* D"? C'mon—that just makes it harder to guess. But as you've already figured out, life is more complicated than a multiple-choice question. If you're trying to decide which friend is going to be your BFF—and the effort of narrowing it down to just one is making your head hurt—then maybe there's more than one right decision. Okay, that may be a silly example. But when you're stumped on a choice, just think about if there could be several ways to answer it. And they could *all* be "correct."

3. DO I NEED TO MAKE THIS DECISION ALONE?
Probably not. And getting some help can be a genius move. The Bible talks a lot about getting advice. Check out this great verse:

> Plans fail for lack of counsel, but with many
> **advisers** they succeed.
>
> (Proverbs 15:22, emphasis added)

God built us to need each other—for support, for love, but also for advice. When "I don't know" is all that's coming out of your brain, think about which wise Jesus-follower could give you some godly advice—or maybe all of the above.

7. BAD DECISION...THEN WHAT? (RECOVERING FROM MISTAKES)

So you've blown it. You made a bad decision—maybe a *really* bad one. We've all been there, so *now* what? Isn't God ticked off when we make a mistake?

The truth is God really does hate sin because sin hurts you and others. BUT GOD'S STILL CRAZY ABOUT YOU! Always has been. Always will be. And there's no mistake you can't overcome. None. Zero. Zip. Nada. Not even the worst one you can think of.

But you have a choice: (1) You can beat yourself up for making a mistake, which doesn't help much, or (2) You can stand up after a bad decision knocks you down. If you choose the second option, then here are some key next steps you can take:

ADMIT IT.

Don't try to cover it up, explain it away, or pretend it didn't happen. Don't minimize it and tell yourself, *Anyone woulda done it* when you KNOW you've made a mistake. The first step to making it better is just to confess it and own up to your part of it.

APOLOGIZE FOR IT.

Yep, we're talking about saying a good old-fashioned "I'm sorry for _____." First, apologize to God because every wrong decision is an insult to God. But it's gotta be more than just words you say—you've gotta feel it. You can tell when someone's apologizing and they don't really mean it, can't you? It has to come from your heart. And if your decision has hurt any people, then you should honestly apologize to them, too. We know it's easier said than done.

ACCEPT FORGIVENESS.

When you've truly apologized, you need to receive the gift of forgiveness. Don't beat yourself up over and over—just accept that an amazing thing has happened. Check this out:

> If we confess our sins, he is faithful and just and will forgive us our sins and purify us from all unrighteousness.
>
> (1 John 1:9)

ASSESS IT.

Evaluate your bad decision. What caused it? Think about how you're going to avoid making the same mistake next time.

These aren't magic steps you take to make yourself feel better, but they *are* important parts of recovering from a bad decision. We've (Marko and Scott) both made more bad decisions than we can count, so you're not alone when you feel like you've messed up. But if you Admit, Apologize, Accept, and Assess (hey, those words all start with A!) you *can* recover from a bad decision.

8. THE FUTURE SEEMS KINDA INTIMIDATING (I STILL WANNA BE A KID)

There's a weird tension most teenagers feel at some point: You want to be grown up, but you still want to be a kid, too. Does that make sense? Like, there are days (or even minutes) when you really want to be grown up—you're totally looking forward to having more freedom and making more of your own decisions and experiencing stuff that you don't get to experience yet.

You also want your friends to think you're all grown up. And you probably want people you don't know (of all ages) to treat you like an older teenager. Doesn't it bug you when older teenagers treat you like a little kid? The last thing you want is to have a cute guy or cute girl treat you like you're younger than you are.

So there's all this pressure to act older and dress older and talk older and be older. The problem is, if you're totally honest (and you might as well be honest—if you can't be honest with a book, then who can you be honest with?), there are times when you just want to be a kid.

There are probably things about being a kid that you're not ready to give up. The future—as cool as it might be—is full of unknowns. The past (being a kid) is something you know and are comfortable with.

Guess what? If what we've been describing here sounds like you, then you're normal. Seriously, most young teenagers want *some* of what it means to grow up, but they also want to hold on to *some* of the comfort of their childhood.

Our advice: Don't rush into growing up. And don't be embarrassed by the "kid stuff" you might still have in your life.

"WHY DO PEOPLE WANT MORE STUFF LIKE CELL PHONES AND CLOTHES WHEN THEY'RE IN JUNIOR HIGH?"
—CONNOR, 6TH GRADE

I WAS A MIDDLE SCHOOL DORK!
—SCOTT

Her name was Wendy. She was the new girl in my seventh-grade social studies class. She had sorta blonde hair and a smile that pulled me in...even though her teeth were hiding behind braces.

As sometimes happens to the new kid in a class, all the popular kids were trying to get Wendy to hang out with their clique. I don't know if Wendy ran with the popular kids at her old school, but at our middle school, everybody wanted to be her friend.

And I'm proud to tell you—Wendy seemed pretty *into* me. Oh yeah.

We weren't boyfriend-girlfriend or anything, but we had a good friendship going. And since this is part of a book called *My Future*, I gotta admit—I was wondering if Wendy and I might have a "future" together. (Ha!)

So one day as I was sitting in social studies class, Mrs. Kommer handed out a test. No sweat—I did pretty well in that class. But partway through the test, I heard a whisper. It was Wendy.

"Hey," she said quietly. "Move your paper so I can see your answers."

Oh, crud.

I'd like to tell you I had a great solution at that moment. But no such luck. I knew that letting her cheat off my test wasn't the right thing to do. But I also knew I wanted Wendy to keep liking me. So...

I moved my paper so she could see it. *Doh!*

Sure, I felt guilty. But I also felt like no real harm had been done (other than CHEATING!). That is, I felt that way until Mrs. Kommer called Wendy out into the hallway the next day. Somebody had snitched. (All these years later, I still have no idea who it was. Maybe some other dude who had a crush on Wendy.)

Five minutes later, Wendy came back into the room, and then Mrs. Kommer called *me* out into the hall. Oh great. As I walked out, Wendy gave me a "look." I knew she was trying to tell me something...but I had no idea what it meant.

So Mrs. Kommer said, "Did you help Wendy cheat yesterday?" Oh, man. She was comparing our stories. Right then I made my first wise choice: I came clean and told the truth. That's the good news.

The bad news is Mrs. Kommer gave me an F on the test. And the other bad news is that Wendy denied that she cheated. So I kinda unknowingly wrecked her story.

How did she respond? Well, let's just say my wife's name is *not* Wendy!

SECTION 3

HIGH SCHOOL

9. HIGH SCHOOL LOOMS AROUND THE CORNER...

In a book about your future, high school really is the "near future." Whether you're all-out excited or a little nervous, high school is definitely on the way. And something is telling you it's not *exactly* like *Friday Night Lights* and *hopefully* not much like *High School Musical*. (Suddenly, we feel like *singing* the rest of this chapter!)

Isn't it strange, though, how so many movies and TV shows are about high school students? There seems to be a fascination with high school. Maybe that's because it can be an incredible time in your life.

But there's a part of you that wonders what it'll be like—higher expectations, more responsibility, parties, upper classmen, initiations, tougher teachers, rumors, dating. Everything hits a new level in high school. Will you be able to handle it all? Will your friends be able to handle it? Will your middle school friends even *be* your friends in high school? What if you don't know what to do? What if you make a fool of yourself? WHAT IF YOU'RE NOT READY?

Well, here's some good news: *You don't have to be ready yet!* Even BETTER news: Middle school is a great practice field for much of what you'll have to deal with during high school.

One of the best pieces of advice we can give you is this: Don't get ahead of yourself! It's easy to start worrying about stuff that's a little ways down the road, but don't do that. Instead, the best thing you can do to get ready for high school is to live wisely today. Scripture is clear on that:

> Therefore do not worry about tomorrow,
> for tomorrow will worry about itself.
> Each day has enough trouble of its own.
>
> (Matthew 6:34)

Yes, high school is coming, and your high school career can be fantastic. (Maybe someone will make a movie or a musical about it.) Just keep doing the best you can while you're still in middle school and keep one eye on the future.

And if you want to take a peek at some specific issues you may run into during the high school years, check out the next few pages.

"HIGH SCHOOL IS GOING TO BE THE BEST TIME OF OUR LIVES!"
—MCCALLISTER, 8TH GRADE

10. ARE THE CLIQUES STILL THERE? GEEKS, JOCKS, AND YOU

Yup, you'll be heading off to high school sometime soon. Depending on what grade you're in now, of course, that could be *very soon* or still a few years away.

One subject lots of middle schoolers ask about is cliques. Part of this question comes from the fact that the cliques you experience in middle school are somewhat new to you. In other words, there weren't cliques—not to the same extreme—when you were in elementary school. Sure, there were friendship groups, and some of them were exclusive (didn't let others in). But they weren't like the ones you're experiencing in middle school.

The reason for the increase in cliques during middle school has to do with how you—and everyone else in your school—are changing. It's actually a brain thing. Since your brain is developing the ability to think in new ways, you're starting to think about yourself in new ways. This is part of discovering your *identity* (a fancy word that just means "who you think you are"). And as you play around with figuring out who you are, you'll start to hang out with people who like the same things you do.

That's what most cliques are—groups of students who are into the same things or at least have something strong in common. Maybe you and your friends like different styles of music, but you're all *really* into something else. Or some cliques define *all kinds* of stuff for you: What music you like, what clothes you wear, how you spend your free time, even what attitude you have.

The short answer to the question in this chapter's title is yes, cliques are even stronger and more fixed in high school. That doesn't mean it's impossible to move between them, but it's more difficult to change friendship groups in high school than it is in middle school.

Here's one thing we've noticed, though: Some of the happiest students in high school are those who don't completely belong to one clique or another, but they move freely between many groups. These students don't let other people define them (as cliques often do); instead, they insist on defining themselves. This gives them a sense of confidence that other students often don't have.

"BE NICE 2 EVERY1, NOT JUST YOUR CLIQUE."
—RYLEIGH, 7TH GRADE

11. WHO'S AT MY LUNCH TABLE? DOES IT MATTER AS MUCH AS IT DOES IN MIDDLE SCHOOL?

Here's a cool thing: High school administrators tend to have fewer rules about where you can be during your lunch period. In most middle schools, you pretty much have to eat your lunch in the cafeteria (or whatever they call the lunch area in your school). But in most high schools, students eat all over the place, gathering with their friends in the cafeteria, on the lawn, in a quad or courtyard, or in some other random place. (Of course, schools located in warmer climates offer more lunchtime location options.)

But "eating all over the place" makes it somewhat more challenging to eat wherever you want. It's a strange thing. This is because certain groups or cliques tend to have their gathering place, and everyone in the school knows it's "the place where that group eats."

Here's something we've noticed over lots of years spent working with teenagers: In middle school, the kids who aren't part of a clique that always sits at the same lunch table are often lonely kids who don't feel like they fit in. That's sometimes true in high school as well, but there are also some of the sharpest and happiest kids in the whole school who don't feel the pressure to eat with a certain group. They're comfortable moving around.

We'll admit, this "Where do I eat lunch?" question is a lot bigger deal than it seems like it should be. We understand (and remember) how important it is to feel like you belong somewhere. That "Where do I belong?" question (which matters more than "Where do I eat lunch?") is an important part of being a teenager. In fact, it's one of the reasons the teenage years exist in the first place.

So we encourage you to think about where you belong. But we also encourage you to hold loosely to whatever answers you come up with. While it's important to have friends, it's also important to leave some room for who you might become.

12. SAT/ACT TESTS

Have you heard of the Scholastic Assessment Test? Most people just call it the SAT (Don't say "sat," say the letters.) Actually, the SAT originally stood for "Scholastic Achievement Test." Then it was changed to "Scholastic Aptitude Test" and *then* "Scholastic Assessment Test." And here's the funny part: After all those changes, the people in charge of creating the test still weren't happy with whatever A-word they used for the middle letter. So they now say that "SAT" doesn't stand for anything—it's just SAT. Okay, whatever.

Have you ever heard of the ACT? (Again, say the letters, not "act.") The letters actually stand for the name of the company that owns it—the American College Testing Program, Incorporated. But everyone just calls it the ACT.

The SAT and ACT are two college-entrance exams. Students hoping to go to college take one (or sometimes both) of these tests; college admissions committees look at students' test scores when they're deciding who can attend their schools. It's not the only thing they use—but it's one of the important things.

Why are there two tests? They're slightly different, and some schools prefer one to the other. In the United States, most schools on the East or West Coast use the SAT, while most schools in the Midwest and South use the ACT. Kind of confusing, huh?

The big question that middle school students ask us about these tests is, *Do I need to start worrying about the SAT or ACT now?* You might get different answers to this question, depending on whom you ask. (This is why there are companies who will try to get your parents' money so they can start preparing you *now* to take one test or the other when you're in high school.) Our opinion—and it's a pretty strong one (we *really* believe this): Don't sweat it now. Don't spend time or energy thinking about the SAT or ACT.

Sure, if you're hoping to go to college, then getting good grades is important. Even in middle school, your grades will impact what classes you can take in high school, which will ultimately make a difference in how colleges view you as a potential student. But the grades you get in your classes don't actually make a difference on your SAT or ACT score. So relax. Do your best in school, sure. But don't start worrying about your SAT or ACT score at this point—wait 'til you're in 10th or 11th grade.

13. ARE HIGH SCHOOL PARTIES AS CRAZY AS I'VE HEARD?

WE KNOW YOU THOUGHT *STEWARDESSES* IS THE LONGEST WORD THAT CAN BE TYPED USING ONLY THE LEFT HAND, BUT WE'RE HERE TO TELL YOU THAT IT'S *AFTERCATARACTS*. (GIVE IT A SHOT!)

This is, like, a trick question...right? Or if it isn't a trick question, then it might seem like including it in this book is a trick of some sort.

We're going to write bluntly and honestly here, okay?

Yes, some high school parties are crazy. Totally crazy. Insanely crazy. But here's the tricky part: *Crazy* means different things in different situations and to different people. If you say, "That chocolate dessert was crazy!" you might mean, "That chocolate dessert was so wonderful and absolutely choco-licious, it's almost impossible to find words for it. So I must call it 'crazy.'" Or you might mean, "Someone put something terrible in that chocolate, so I must call it 'crazy' because anyone who would either make it or eat it must not have all of their mental abilities." See, *crazy* can be good or bad.

A crazy high school party can be both of those (no, not choco-licious). Lots of high school kids have a bit too much freedom, and their parents let them do some truly crazy things. (In that sentence, *crazy* means "nuts," "loco," "idiotic.") So some of the stuff that happens at parties hosted by kids in that situation is totally out of control. There are definitely high school students who think this kind of party is *crazy*, meaning "fun" and "wild" and "off the hook." The problem is there are *often* negative results and consequences that go along with these kinds of crazy parties.

At the risk of sounding like parents—which, um, we are—here's the deal: If you were in high school, we wouldn't tell you to stay away from every single party. But we *would* tell you it's tough to live as a Jesus follower when you're hanging out at parties. You have to have a great sense of self-control and a ton of maturity.

But you're *not* in high school. And if you care about our advice at all, then we'd encourage you to totally stay away from high school parties at this age. Really, you need to use wisdom even when you're choosing which middle school parties you'll attend. Remember: When you put yourself into situations where people are making lousy choices, it's just that much easier to make a choice you'll regret.

14. INDEPENDENCE: CAN I REALLY HAVE MORE OF IT IN HIGH SCHOOL?

In our conversations with middle school students, one thing we often hear is that they really wish their parents wouldn't treat them like little kids anymore. Can anyone relate to that? (We can picture you nodding your head.)

"C'MON, MOM! I'm not seven years old anymore!"

Maybe there's a rule in your house that kind of made sense when you were younger, but not anymore. Or maybe your parents treat you in a way that was okay when you were in third grade, but now you're a teenager, right? (Or almost a teenager, anyway.)

Well, there's a secret that can be the fast track to more independence—and it'll go a long way toward your parents treating you *more* like an older person and less like a little kid.

THE SECRET: Your parents will almost certainly give you more independence when they see you're maturing. But the flip side is true, too: If they don't see it, then they probably ain't givin' it.

It's easy to think that just because you're moving from middle school into high school you'll automatically get more independence. But it's not a gimme. Usually, independence is something you have to prove you deserve. Luckily (whether or not you know it), you've already been showing your parents that you deserve more independence.

It's like this: When you were little, your parents wouldn't let you go into the bathroom alone—probably because they thought you might drink the toilet water. They wouldn't let you open the refrigerator by yourself because you might pull the carton of eggs and the ketchup and last night's leftovers onto the kitchen floor. There were all kinds of things they wouldn't let you do because you hadn't proven to them that you could handle it.

WE INTERRUPT THIS CHAPTER FOR A SPECIAL NEWS ALERT: Your parents are now waiting for you to prove you can handle it. And there's a pretty cool reward for your efforts: MORE INDEPENDENCE.

Grab your Bible and check out Ephesians 6:1-2. This passage says it's important that you not only *obey* your parents, but also *honor* them. That means *how* you interact with them is just as important as doing what they ask you to do. (You know, the famous "attitude conversation.") You don't always have to agree with them, but Scripture says you do have to honor them. And when you do it God's way, you'll see your independence increase.

Give it a try and you'll see what we mean. (But still—no drinking toilet water, okay?)

15. CAN I "BE COOL" AND STILL FOLLOW JESUS IN HIGH SCHOOL?

The Pursuit of Cool. It happens in middle school, doesn't it? But it's different than it was in elementary school. Sure, even little kids get a sense of who's cool or popular—but what does it really mean? Let's define *popular* or *cool* as "being widely liked and approved of."

Question: Is there anything wrong with the desire to be liked and approved of? Of course not! You see, God *made* us to be in relationship with other people. Check out Genesis 2. Here humankind ran into its first-ever problem—even before sin came on the scene.

> The Lord God said, "It is not good for the man to be alone."
>
> (Genesis 2:18)

In our desire to be with people, we want to be liked. That's part of how God wired us. But sometimes that desire to be liked takes over. That's when it goes beyond just wanting to be accepted and goes all the way to wanting to be on top—to be the best. When this happens, the desire for meaningful friendships becomes less important than wanting to be cool (or at least *look* cool).

How do you know if the pull of popularity is reaching up to grab you by the throat? Here are some warning signs:

- You stand in front of your closet for long periods of time, *worrying* about what clothes will look right.

- You regularly walk into school thinking, *What will people think?* over and over again.

- You often decide not to include someone who wants to hang out with you because you think doing so will make *you* less popular.

Our level of cool or popularity is often determined by how we look or how we appear. But God's definition of *cool* is more about what we do—especially the way we treat people. Philippians 2:3-4 (NLT) says:

Don't be selfish; don't try to impress others.

Be humble, thinking of others as better than yourselves.

Don't look out only for your own interests, but take an interest in others, too.

That's *God's* definition of cool. And when you think about it, who wouldn't agree with that? If you meet someone who treats you like this passage says (read it again really quick), then you're bound to think that person is fantastically COOL!

16. MY REPUTATION: WHAT EXACTLY IS IT AND CAN SOMEONE WRECK IT?

Picture someone at your school or in your town you've never actually met, but you know something about the person. Do you have an opinion about her?

If you do, then it probably comes from her reputation. *Reputation* basically means "a public opinion." But reputations can be misleading because people often have different opinions about something or someone.

You probably don't personally know any Hollywood celebrities, but you know their reputations. What's your favorite actor or singer like in private? Well, what you know is basically what you've *heard* about them.

Now let's think about *your* reputation using these questions:

IF ALL PEOPLE HAVE THEIR OWN OPINIONS, THEN WHO DECIDES WHAT SOMEONE'S REPUTATION IS?
Good question. A reputation usually forms out of what most people (or at least the most outspoken people) think about a person. There could be lots of people who think highly of a particular celebrity, but maybe there are even more people who don't have such a great opinion of that celeb. Your reputation usually comes from what *most* people say about you (but not always).

SO IS MY REPUTATION JUST UP TO OTHER PEOPLE?

Yes...and no. Even though some people could have inaccurate opinions about you, your actions really *do* influence those opinions. For instance, if you spend a lot of time at parties, you may earn the reputation as a partier. So even though part of your reputation is based on opinions, some of it can be based on facts, too.

IN HIGH SCHOOL, CAN SOMEONE WRECK MY REPUTATION?

Well, that's a complicated question. If someone wants to damage a movie star's reputation, he might spread lies and rumors about her. (Check out the next·chapter for more on that.) And gossip sells more magazines, whether or not it's based on truth. Someone could also tell lies about *you*, so it's possible that your reputation could take a hit. But the source of the information has to be considered, too.

BUT MORE IMPORTANT THAN YOUR REPUTATION IS WHAT'S *TRUE* ABOUT YOU.

You can control only *yourself.* If people tell lies about you, then remember that the truth will eventually come out. So instead of *worrying so much* about what people think of you, you've got to focus on who you're becoming.

Your reputation always takes a backseat to who you *really* are—no matter what people say.

"REPUTATIONS AREN'T THE MOST IMPORTANT THINGS IN THE WORLD, BUT YOU DON'T WANT TO BE KNOWN AS A PERSON WHO DOESN'T MEAN WHAT SHE SAYS."

—KAYLA, 7TH GRADE

17. "I HEARD A RUMOR"

You'll hear rumors dozens of times (well, probably hundreds or even thousands of times) over the next few years. You'll especially hear them a bunch when you're just about to start high school and also when you're the new kid in school.

> "I heard a rumor that there's an old swimming pool underneath the gym floor."

> "I heard a rumor that the custodian got arrested for murder but the charges were dropped."

> "I heard a rumor that the seniors make the freshmen run naked through the showers and snap them with wet towels."

Ooh—and it's even worse when the things you hear don't have the "I heard a rumor" preface:

> "You know that stuff they serve at lunch that's covered in gravy? It's cat."

> "In high school they'll kick you out for frowning. It's their new zero-tolerance rule."

> "There's a kid at our school who's 25 years old. He keeps getting held back."

Here's some advice that could really help you for the rest of your life, but especially as you head to high school: *Don't believe everything you hear.* Yeah, we know we're not the first ones to say it.

But it's still good advice. Being "skeptical" (not believing everything you hear) is a valuable thing. The Bible even praises a group of people called the Bereans (say buh-REE-uns) for being skeptical about what the Bible teachers of their time were telling them (see Acts 17:10-12).

Most rumors are false. Don't waste your time with 'em.

"RUMORS...THEY HURT. DON'T DO IT.
HOW WOULD YOU FEEL IF IT WERE [SAID] ABOUT YOU?"
—LEIGH, 7TH GRADE

18. FEAR OF "FRESHMAN INITIATIONS"

The upperclassmen constantly pound on the freshmen.

They also make the freshmen dissect live gerbils in science class when the teacher isn't looking.

No, seriously, every single ninth-grade guy has to wear his underwear on his head in the locker room.

Yeah, and every single ninth-grade girl is forced to kiss that ugly statue in the school lobby.

The previous chapter covered rumors about high school. This one takes it a bit further to address rumors about freshman initiations. These rumors seem to be in all parts of the country.

First, do you know what an *initiation* (say in-ish-ee-AY-shun) is? It's a test or ceremony that someone goes through to formally join a group. Like, you could say an army recruit's boot camp is an initiation. Or even that an orientation day for new students is an initiation.

But normally when the word is used, people think of initiations that aren't quite as "official"— like when college students are joining fraternities (guys) or sororities (girls) and are pressured to do humiliating stuff to "prove" their commitment. (This is also sometimes called "hazing.")

Now back to the rumors about initiations for high school freshmen. There are *tons* of rumors about this stuff, and *almost all of them* are totally false. However, there probably *will be* times when you feel like the older students are looking down on you—that does seem to be a pretty normal freshman experience.

And, of course, there are bullies everywhere—no matter how old you are. So it's possible that you'll have to deal with someone bullying you as well.

But in general, the wild rumors you hear about freshman initiations are no truer than the legends of the Loch Ness Monster, Big Foot, the Abominable Snowman, or alien abductions.

19. IS EVERY HIGH SCHOOL STUDENT REALLY HAVING SEX?

You've probably had the sex education class in which lots of giggling happened. (Come on, we've been there. Actually, we may have been the ones cracking jokes.) Maybe you're real curious about the topic. Or you may wonder what all the ruckus is about.

Or maybe you've done some experimenting of your own—more than you wish you had. But you've seen movies and TV shows with high school guys and girls hooking up. Those kinds of images mess with your mind. BTW, did you know that the "high school" actors and actresses you watch usually aren't teenagers? It's true!

So, is *every* high school kid really having sex?

The quick answer? Nope. In fact, surveys show that *fewer than half* of high school students have "done it." And that fact makes this next statement also true: *Most* high school students *aren't* having sex.

That's important to know, because when you believe everyone is doing something, there's often a little voice inside you that asks, *Should I be doing that, too?*

This chapter isn't meant to tell you about all the dangers that go along with having sex in high school. There's a ton of info out there about all the big risks involved. So we're gonna assume you've probably heard them by now. What we *do* want to emphasize here is that the claim "everyone's doing it" is just plain baloney. Pure and simple.

Statistics say that over the last 15 years, the percentage of high school students having sex has actually *dropped* about 13 percent. More and more high school students are realizing that having sex before marriage is simply risky, dangerous—and just unwise. God designed sex as an amazing experience for a husband and wife to share. Trust God's plan on this one.

What's crazy is this: While the number of real-life high school students having sex has *decreased*, the number of sex scenes on TV has *increased*. And sometimes what we watch on television can seem "normal" or "expected." So think twice about what you see and believe.

But know this:

Everyone's NOT doing it!

And that's a real good thing.

SECTION 4

DATING
RELATIONSHIPS

20. I'M WORRIED ABOUT DATING

Her name was Cindy, and she was the best kick-ball player in my sixth-grade class—no doubt. That's what attracted me (Scott) to her and gave me that weird feeling in my stomach. (You know, like you want to throw up—but in a *good* way, which doesn't make much sense.)

My buddies knew I liked Cindy, and they teased me about it—often. "She's your girlfriend, man!" Well, I definitely liked her. But I knew nothing about girlfriends and dating. Maybe even less than nothing. And I must admit that I worried about it.

GOOD NEWS

It's normal to worry about dating. It's new territory, and it can be a complicated thing because *people* are complicated—after all, they're the ones who date. It might help to remember that you're not the only one who's nervous about it. (You might be the only one who's *admitting* you're worried, but that's another story.)

MORE GOOD NEWS

Everybody's learning about dating at the same time—but at a different pace. Sure, some of your friends might have learned a few things from watching their older brothers or sisters date. (I learned a little bit from my older brother. But years later, he told me he didn't know what he was doing back then, either. Great.) Still, it's pretty common for some people to exaggerate how much they really know about it. Don't let them intimidate you!

IMPORTANT FACT

When you're thinking about when to start dating, realize that everybody's timetable is different. Even if your friends are way into it already, take the pressure off and don't let other people stress you out about it, either. Friends of mine tried to make plans for Cindy and me, but I was just fine with giving her a high-five after she launched the kickball for another home run.

One idea that's really worth considering is talking with one of your parents (or another adult you trust) about your dating worries. Don't roll your eyes—it really can help! Maybe start out like this: "Mom and Dad, I want to talk to you about something, but I don't want you to freak out on me. Can you promise me that?" If they say yes, then ask them if they can remember what they were thinking about when they started to wonder about dating.

Remember, God made you—including your desire to spend time with the opposite sex—and you're not the only one who's figuring it out (even though it probably feels that way sometimes).

21. WHAT IF I NEVER HAVE A DATE?

Some teenagers don't care about dating at all. Others care about it *way too much*. And most are, of course, somewhere in the middle—they'd like to date, maybe have a few dates during high school, but they aren't obsessed with it.

Girls tend to think about dating more than guys do. Some of that's just biology (guys think about sex more; girls think about romance and relationships more). But some of it is stuff we've picked up from our culture—what TV shows and movies and magazines and friends say is "normal."

That cultural thing (what TV shows and movies and magazines and other kids say is "normal") can be a really big pressure at times. It's easy to believe you're "not normal" if you don't have a boyfriend or girlfriend, or if you aren't going on dates all the time. But here's something that's super-important to understand: Culture lies to us all the time and about all kinds of stuff. And our culture's lies about dating are just one example of this.

Ready for the facts? Studies show that just barely half of all high school students actually date. And only a third have a boyfriend or girlfriend. Have you figured it out yet? That means it's *normal* not to date! And it's *really normal* not to have a boyfriend or girlfriend! In fact, you might say that teenagers who *do have* boyfriends or girlfriends aren't normal.

Here's our encouragement to you: Part of figuring out who you are and how you fit in with the world is getting to know teenagers of the other gender. But the best way to do that, while avoiding all of the weird pressures of dating (not to mention all the pressure to do physical stuff that you'll end up regretting), is to "group date." This just means hanging out with a group of guys and girls. Group dating isn't romantic, and it doesn't involve couples hooking up. It's just a mixed-gender group doing stuff together.

So while a date can be a nice thing, and it's fun to have those "Ooh, I think I *really like* this person" feelings, it's much better to hang out with a group of friends—including some of the opposite gender.

"ALL MY FRIENDS ARE DATING. I DON'T KNOW WHAT TO DO!"
—ROBYN, 7TH GRADE

22. I'M NOT SURE I'D EVEN KNOW WHAT TO *DO* ON A DATE

Think about it: Everybody goes on a "first date." That's probably why there are so many hilarious movies containing really awkward date scenes—it's something just about every person can relate to.

Most everyone we know has at least one story about a really uncomfortable date. For example, in college I (Scott) went on a first date with Tracy, a really cute redhead. We were studying together (exciting date, huh?), and I had my feet propped up on a table while I was reading my book. You know how sometimes gas needs to escape from your body, and it kind of surprises you? Well, it surprised me. And from the look on Tracy's face, I'm guessing it surprised her, too. Hey, are you laughing at me? I was embarrassed!

You know, dating is really all about friendship—enjoying just being with someone. So if you're spending time with someone you kinda like and doing something fun, then you're on your way to a good date.

Do you want more specific tips? Here you go:

DON'T BE IN A BIG HURRY TO "PAIR OFF" WITH SOMEONE.

One-on-one dating can be awkward, especially when you're first starting to date. Plus, if you really want to grow a friendship with someone, then you can do that while a bunch of your friends are around. Group dates are a *great* way to get to know a guy or a girl you like. Go bowling, mini-golfing, to the beach or pool—go anywhere that a group of people would go to have fun. Too often, students imagine "dating" as being two people sitting on a couch and stuttering for the next thing to say while sweat pours off their foreheads because they're so worried about looking like a dork. Take the pressure off. One-on-one dating will come more naturally after you get to know someone as part of a larger group.

EXPECT A LITTLE AWKWARDNESS SOMETIMES.

Guys and girls naturally separate from each other in elementary school, and they kind of "rediscover" each other as they move into their teenage years. When you were first learning how to ride a bike, you probably crashed a few times, right? Well, it's likely that you'll crash a few times as you figure out how to date, too. So don't worry if you're not such a smooth operator in the beginning. And look at it this way—you'll have some funny stories to tell later on. (Just ask Tracy.)

NEVER LET A GUY OR A GIRL PRESSURE YOU INTO DOING SOMETHING THAT MAKES YOU UNCOMFORTABLE.

If your date tries to push you to do something that you're not ready to do, be confident enough to say no. You can be sure that type of person is *not* who you want to be dating.

Bottom line? Remember, dating is ultimately about friendship. So relax and have fun! (And keep your feet off the table.)

23. HOW DOES MY PHYSICAL SELF AFFECT MY DATING?

What makes someone "attractive" to date? Wow—there's no simple answer for that one. This much is true: Your "physical self" plays a role—it makes the first impression on someone. So if you walk into a room and you look dirty, you smell like Taco Bell, or you have birds nesting in your hair, then people will decide stuff about you. (Like, you really need to take a shower.) In a culture that focuses so much on *image*, what you look like can easily be overemphasized. But—right or wrong—your physical appearance is a first clue to someone.

As we mentioned in the last chapter, dating is about *way* more than physical attraction. It's really about friendship and character. It's more about w*ho you are* than how you look. Have you heard the expression "beauty is in the eye of the beholder"? It basically means that real attractiveness is *personal*. Do you know any older couples who seem to be crazy about each other? I recently watched an online video about a couple celebrating 80 years of marriage. EIGHTY! They were more wrinkled than a pair of old baseball gloves, but I could tell they're still in love. Where does that kind of long-lasting attraction come from?

I think couples like the one I saw in that video see each other kind of like the way God sees us. God knows way more about us than just how we look. Check out 1 Samuel 16:7: "People look at the **outward appearance**, but the Lord looks at the heart" (emphasis added). Yet God has an advantage—he can immediately see right into our hearts, but it takes *time* for us to get to know someone else's heart.

We're not saying you should ignore how you look. Take care of your body. Be healthy. Don't be a slob. Take a shower. Get some of that three-week-old grit out from underneath your fingernails. But don't obsess over your physical appearance—especially if it keeps you from paying attention to what's going on inside of you.

Think of it this way: What if a candy company used the coolest wrappers, but the candy was made of dried glue? You'd take one bite and spit it out. Well, some people spend all their time improving their "packaging" instead of increasing the quality of the candy. If you're constantly focused on how you look, then you'll probably end up dating someone who's only interested in what you look like—not in who you really are inside.

So if you want to hang out with someone who cares about more than just your "wrapper," then pay attention to growing your heart.

I WAS A MIDDLE SCHOOL DORK!
—MARKO

Oh, man, I can hardly believe I'm going to share this one with you. It's one of the most embarrassing moments of my life, and I've hardly ever shared it with anyone. But here I am, typing it out for thousands of middle school readers to see.

So. The summer before ninth grade, I went on a two-week wilderness trip with a bunch of kids from my church youth group. We joined dozens of other kids from other churches, and we were split into groups for the whole two weeks. I wasn't with any of my friends, but it was still an amazing time. Except for one really bad, embarrassing moment.

We were a good week into the trip, and we'd spent the day canoeing down a beautiful river in the Appalachian Mountains—far from any towns. We had to find a place to camp for the night, and then we'd continue canoeing the next day.

Our group came across a nice warm sandbar in the middle of the river (a fast one with strong currents), and we wanted to camp on the sandbar. Our group leader didn't think it was a good idea because she wouldn't allow us to go to the bathroom on the sandbar (because "it" could eventually seep into the river). She warned us that if we camped on the sandbar, we'd have to forge the river and walk into the woods in order to go to the bathroom.

We insisted it wouldn't be a problem, and we set up camp on the sandbar. It was soft for sleeping, and the sand was still warm from the day's sun. We were happy. I was happy—at least until sometime during the middle of the night.

Now comes the part where I have to choose my words carefully. Whether from the food or the nervousness of being outside or even from the laziness of not wanting to dig a hole every time I had to "relieve myself," I hadn't gone to the bathroom all week (the squatting kind, that is, not the standing kind). But around 2 or 3 in the morning, I sat up straight in my sleeping bag, and I knew I had only a few minutes until I was going to be in trouble, if you know what I mean.

The thought of forging the river in the middle of the night sounded horrible. And everyone was sleeping and would never know (I told myself). So, right on that sandbar (with NO trees or bushes around), I dug a little hole and started to do my business.

I have no idea what woke everyone up, but that's exactly what they all did. And I was caught in the midst of my "act" in plain sight of everyone. It wasn't pretty, except that it was pretty embarrassing!

24. TO GO OR NOT TO GO?

WAIT! Don't skip this section! Some of you answered this "to go or not to go" question *way* too fast.

This might be your thought process:

School?	"Ugh."
College?	"Sounds like going to school by *choice*."
My choice?	"I want to be done with school!"

Sure, college isn't for everyone. But before you start dreaming about no more textbooks, or crazy teachers, or boring lectures, or brain-numbing homework, you should consider a couple of things.

COLLEGE CAN HELP YOU GET (AND KEEP) A GREAT JOB SOMEDAY.

As our world keeps growing and changing and as technologies advance, college is an important tool. Maybe you're thinking you're not a real "books" person. That's cool. I have a friend who'd say he's more of a video-game person than a book person. In fact, his *job* is making new video games for a well-known video game company. But he wouldn't have the training he needs to do that job without a college degree.

ON AVERAGE, PEOPLE WHO GO TO COLLEGE EARN MORE MONEY.

Now, hopefully you already realize that there are way more important things in the world than money. But it's not a bad thing to be able to get a job that puts dollars in your pocket. Not just so you can spend money on yourself or on your family, but so you can invest in God's work in the world and help people who really need it. *That's* an awesome feeling!

WHAT ABOUT A GREAT CAREER THAT DOESN'T REQUIRE A COLLEGE DEGREE?

There are plenty of those, too. We know some terrific, smart people who have amazing and fulfilling jobs even though they didn't go to college. But their secret seems to be this: They were already working *toward* a specific passion or career—not running *away* from college.

Middle school isn't too early to start thinking about college. It's actually the perfect time to begin thinking about it because you don't have the "pressure" of making a decision right away. Once again, this is a great area to talk about with someone you respect. If it's on your mind, then track down a person who cares about you and ask him what he thinks. We bet he'd love to talk with you.

> "IF YOU HAVE THE OPPORTUNITY TO LEARN, YOU SHOULD DO IT BECAUSE IT'S A PRIVILEGE, AND BECAUSE PLENTY OF PEOPLE CAN'T."
>
> —JASMIN, 8TH GRADE

25. PICKING THE "RIGHT" ONE

If you're thinking about which college to attend, then you're already ahead of the game—so congratulate yourself. Give yourself a pat on the back. Go ahead, we'll wait. Honestly, it's great if you have your eyes on a college already. But you're a long way off from having to commit to a university.

Or maybe you feel like someone you know has a head start because she already knows where she wants to go to college, but you haven't given it a thought. Well, maybe she'll end up a "Spartan" or a "Bruin"; but then again, maybe she won't. A friend who lived next door to me in junior high insisted that he was going to go to Purdue University "because they develop the best quarterbacks." But when the time came, he ended up going...somewhere that wasn't Purdue. And he loved it!

No matter where you are on the "picking a college" timetable, there are some great things you can start thinking about now.

WHAT CAREER DO YOU THINK YOU MIGHT LIKE? AND WHAT SCHOOLS OFFER A GOOD PROGRAM FOR THAT CAREER?

If you don't know what kind of career you might want—don't sweat it. But if you know you like architecture, or teaching, or arts, or languages, or science, then check into which colleges have a good program in your area(s) of interest.

WHAT *SIZE* SCHOOL DO YOU THINK YOU MIGHT LIKE TO ATTEND?

There are plenty of great small colleges you've probably never even heard of. But both big and small colleges can be fantastic. Be open to all the options.

THERE ARE *LOTS* OF RESOURCES THAT CAN HELP YOU WHENEVER YOU'RE READY.

You'll find them online as well as through your school's counselors, your parents, and your friends. You don't have to make this important choice without help.

On the flip side, here are some not-so-smart ways to choose the "right" college:

- A girl you like says *she* might go there.

- The college has a hilarious mascot costume.

- The school colors go really well with your eyes.

- It's close to your favorite mall.

Finally, be assured that if you head to college and find out it really isn't the "right" one for you, there's always time to make an adjustment. You can do some further exploring and find what's best for you.

26. WORRYING ABOUT COLLEGE

Really, college is a *long way off.* Don't waste your brain cells and emotional energy by worrying about it now.

Sure, if you're thinking of becoming a doctor or pursuing some other kind of job that requires lots of hard time in college, then you should be careful about your schoolwork and grades, even now. But there's still no reason to *worry* about college.

Here's some advice that's easier to hear than it is to do. (Actually, it's easier to say than it is to do, and we don't always do it, either.) Don't worry! Worry never changes anything. Worrying about anything—college, grades, friends, dating, high school, health, tests, whatever—doesn't fix that thing or guarantee it will be okay. All worry does is make you stressed and sometimes sick.

So, to be totally honest, that saying ("worry never changes anything") isn't completely true. Worry does change one thing: You. It makes you grumpy and cranky, nervous and sad. And those emotions ultimately change you.

You can't control whether or not worry shows up in your life, but you *can* control how you respond when it does. Notice it. (Think to yourself, *Oh, I'm feeling worried.*) Then choose what you'll do with that feeling. Often, the best response is to ignore it and dismiss it—don't give it any power in your life. In Matthew 6:27, Jesus says, "Can any one of you by worrying add a single hour to your life?" Basically, Jesus is saying, "Chill!"

Another good response to worry is taking action—do something that addresses whatever it is you're worried about. Like, if you're worried about a test, then you could study for it.

As a young teenager, there's not much you can do about college now. So we'll say it again—don't waste your time worrying about it.

27. WHAT EXACTLY IS A "MAJOR" AND HOW DO I PICK ONE?

What's your favorite subject in school? Math? English? Science? Social studies? Art? Gym?

Now imagine being able to focus most of your learning time around that one subject. That's kind of what happens when you pick a major in college. A *major* is simply "the subject area of focus" in which you get your college degree. If you've ever heard someone say, "Bob has a degree in education," for example, that just means education (teaching) was his major.

When you graduate from high school, you receive a diploma, right? But it's kind of an "all-purpose" diploma. It's the same diploma for the guy who likes math, or the girl who loves shop class, or the guy who didn't like any of his classes and spent most of his time sleeping and drooling on his desk, yet somehow graduated.

But colleges don't give out diplomas that don't name a major. That's why when it's time to start looking for a college (it's not time yet—read the last two chapters if you haven't already), it's helpful to know what you'd like to study, because some schools offer better programs for certain majors.

I can hear your questions now...

"WHAT IF I DON'T HAVE ANY IDEA WHAT MY MAJOR SHOULD BE?"

The short answer: No worries—you're still in middle school. Answers to questions like this one can definitely wait. And so can the answers to questions like, "How many kids do I want to have?" and "What breakfast cereal will be my favorite when I'm 21?" You don't have to know that stuff yet.

"WHEN I PICK A MAJOR, DOES THAT 'LOCK ME IN'? OR CAN I CHANGE MY MIND?"

Well, sorry. When you pick a major, that's the subject you *must* love with all of your heart for the next 50 years. Just kidding! Lots of people change their majors during college. In fact *more than half* of all college students change their majors at least once. Scott did. Marko didn't. His major was "Music Enjoyment and Hanging Out." (Well, not officially!)

"WHEN I GRADUATE WITH A DEGREE IN A CERTAIN MAJOR, DOES THAT MEAN THAT'S THE ONLY KIND OF JOB I CAN GET?"

Not at all! Many people get a degree in one subject but end up doing something completely different. And while lots of youth pastors have a degree in youth ministry, I (Scott) got a degree in business. It didn't stop me from becoming a youth pastor, though.

Picking a major can make college more enjoyable. You'll be able to study the stuff you REALLY like—and let other people study the stuff you don't.

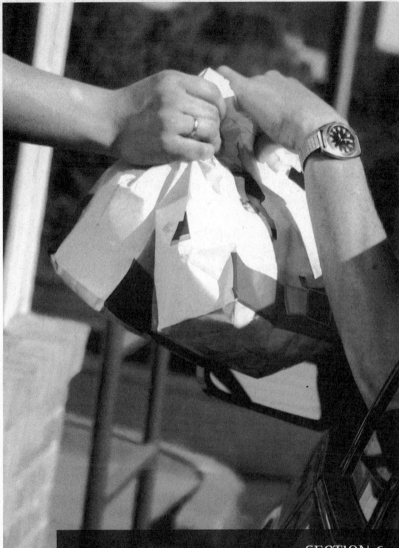

SECTION 6

JOBS/CAREERS

28. HOW DID GOD WIRE ME?

When it comes to thinking about what kind of job or career you might like to pursue, the first thing to think about is...you!

Right now, walk over to the bathroom mirror (or any mirror, for that matter). C'mon—just do it. We'll wait.

Okay, now take a look in the mirror—but not at your hair or that zit or that great shirt you're wearing. Look into your eyes. What's *in* there...deep inside? Do you realize—we mean, *really* realize—that you have your own, unique "wiring"?

You've probably heard someone say that everyone's unique. Everyone is special. Well, it's true! It's not just something a purple dinosaur said when you were little. Everyone's wired a little differently. So what exactly does that mean? Let's break it into three areas:

WHAT STUFF ARE YOU NATURALLY GOOD AT?

Ever since you were little, maybe you've always understood science. Or writing. Or creating stuff. Or mechanical things. Your friends and teachers said, "You're really great at that!" and you thought, *Huh! I never gave it a lot of thought. It just comes naturally to me.*

WHAT STUFF HAVE YOU PRACTICED?

Maybe you play a musical instrument. Or you draw or act or paint or play sports. Those are the more obvious things that you could practice. But you might also practice something without realizing it, like editing your own movies on a computer, writing, leading people, taking stuff apart, or teaching little kids. Look at the activities you've been drawn to—those will give you some great clues.

WHAT STUFF DO YOU REALLY LIKE?

Sometimes people call this a "passion." (More on that in a later chapter.) Maybe your passion is being around animals or fixing cars or helping people or watching the Weather Channel or traveling. It's probably something you spend lots of time thinking about.

For these three areas (the stuff you're good at, the stuff you've practiced, and the stuff you like), write a couple of words that come to mind for each one. Then ask someone you respect to tell you what *she* thinks your gifts and passions are. Lots of times other people can see great stuff in us that we just take for granted.

Now look back at the mirror. That person staring back at you *is* unique. And identifying your unique parts can help point you toward a job you'll love doing someday.

29. WHAT SHOULD I BE WHEN I GROW UP?

When we (Marko and Scott) were little kids (you're probably thinking, *Wasn't that in, like, medieval times?*), we dreamed of being astronauts. People had just started landing on the moon, and it was a wild and crazy dream to think we might get to do that someday. (Fireman was the other kiddy dream job back then.)

But then when I (Marko) got to middle school and high school, I started thinking I might enjoy being an architect or an engineer of some sort because I really like drafting (technical drawing). The problem is I stink at math, and engineers and architects have to be really good at math.

It's cool to have dreams about what job you might have someday. Since God made you a unique person with skills and desires and a personality like no one else's, it makes sense that you'd think some jobs sound cooler than others. And, really, that's a great place to start—even at your age. What do you really love to do? What subjects in school get you cranked and excited? What do you hate or dislike? When it comes to thinking about a future job and career, your likes and dislikes (all part of God's special creation of you) are a perfect place to start.

But there's more to it than that. There's a much deeper issue to consider—no job, as perfect as it might be for your likes and dislikes, will ever make you happy. Happiness—real, deep contentment—is an inner thing that doesn't always have much to do with your job. It's pretty easy to find trash collectors who are deeply happy. And it's pretty easy to find rock stars, millionaire businesspeople, and even architects and engineers who are deeply *unhappy*.

That's because happiness isn't really tied to what you do. Sure, a job you love can make a big difference in how you feel about yourself and about your life, just like a job you hate can make a big difference. But, really, happiness has to do with whether or not you feel connected to God and connected, in a meaningful way, to the people you love.

So go ahead and dream about what job you might want to do someday. But spend more time dreaming about how you can deeply connect with the God who loves you and with the people who'll be your deep, lifelong friends and companions.

MEL BLANC (THE VOICE OF BUGS BUNNY) HATED CARROTS—ESPECIALLY RAW ONES.

30. SCHOOL MATTERS (FOR YOUR FUTURE JOB)

You've probably heard—from parents or teachers or school counselors—that it's important to get good grades (or to do well in school) if you want to have the job of your dreams someday. There's some truth to this, but it's not the whole story. It depends on what you want to do. Like, if you want to become a doctor, then school really matters. But if you want to become a chef, well, getting great grades in algebra doesn't matter quite as much.

But here's the reality: Ten or 15 years from now, almost *no one* your age will have the careers they expected—or even wanted—to have when they were in middle school. You're in this crazy time of change. Everything's changing: Your body, how you think, your emotions, your relationships, your understanding of the world. So in the middle of all that change—which will continue for a few more years, at least—it's not a great idea to make big assumptions about what job you'll end up doing when you grow up.

This is where school becomes important for everyone:

FIRST, SCHOOL IS IMPORTANT BECAUSE IT KEEPS YOUR OPTIONS OPEN.

Do you know what it means to "keep your options open"? It means you don't make decisions that will eliminate one of your options. Like, when it comes to making a decision about what color to paint your bedroom, keeping your options open means you consider all colors, not just one. Here's another example: Let's say you decide, "Hey, I want to be a professional cat juggler when I grow up. So school doesn't really matter; only juggling and cats are important to me now." Since you don't care about school, you end up getting lousy grades and really limiting your career options. After all, in 10 years it would be pretty difficult to suddenly say, "Oops! Now I want to be a lawyer."

SECOND, SCHOOL IS A SUPER-IMPORTANT PART OF *HELPING* YOU FIGURE OUT WHAT YOU MIGHT WANT TO DO SOMEDAY.

As you cruise or struggle your way through math and science and writing and tons of other subjects, you have a cool opportunity to learn more about yourself and how you're wired. Here's an example: I (Marko) really liked geometry (math about shapes), but I struggled with algebra (math about equations and logic). That helped me realize I'd probably like a job that had something to do with design or graphics.

So keep your options open. And use your classes as a way to learn more about yourself and how you're unique.

31. MCJOBS: EARLY JOBS YOU'LL NEVER FORGET

I (Marko) had a ton of jobs as a kid and a teenager. By the time I graduated from high school, I'd already:

- Worked in a greenhouse, planting tiny plants

- Had two newspaper delivery routes

- Babysat a bunch, including a full-time job one summer

- Cleaned an office every week for a couple of years

- Washed dishes in a Chinese restaurant

- Delivered flyers for a real estate agent

- Worked for a guy who made custom license plates for cars

- Had three different jobs as a draftsman making drawings for engineering companies

It was nice to have some money of my own during my teenage years. But when I look back on these jobs, their real value didn't come from the money I earned. I was learning all kinds of important stuff.

See, here's the deal: We're all constantly learning, whether we mean to or not. You're learning as you read this book. You learn a little something in every conversation you have. You learn a little something when you walk down the street. You don't learn only when someone's trying to teach you or when you're trying to learn. You're always taking in information and watching things, and those things are shaping your life.

So a job flipping burgers or emptying trash cans might not seem like it's preparing you for the job you want to have someday. But it can teach you all kinds of other important stuff, like:

- How to interact with a boss

- How to interact with coworkers you don't like

- The importance of being on time

- The importance of being responsible and doing what you've agreed to do

- And lots more

All that learning will be really helpful when you set out to get a job you'll really like.

> "IT'S FUN TO GET MONEY FROM A JOB BECAUSE YOU CAN SPEND IT AT STARBUCKS."
>
> —KELLY, 8TH GRADE

32. HOW DO I MAKE ENOUGH MONEY? HOW MUCH IS "ENOUGH"?

Did you read chapter 31 about "McJobs"? If you didn't, then go back and read it before you read this one.

Here's why that last chapter is important: *How much you make* from a job during middle school or high school isn't as important as *what you learn from it.*

But maybe you're not wondering about how much money you'll make in high school. Maybe you're wondering how much money you'll make when you're into your first post-college career. We (Marko and Scott) know middle school students wonder about this—partly because some of them tell us they're wondering about it, but also because so many middle school students talk about the kind of life they want to have someday (which usually means the kind of stuff—house, car, toys—they'll have).

Listen, we won't pretend that how much money you make doesn't matter. We both have jobs, and we want to be paid an amount that's fair. Jesus even said, "Workers deserve their wages" (Luke 10:7).

But we also know—because we've seen it over and over and over again—that in the long run a big salary doesn't make you happy and a small salary doesn't make you miserable.

Sure, there are parts of life that are less complicated if you can afford certain basics like a place to live and food to eat. But after the basics, money complicates things. From what we can tell, it's actually *more diffi- cult* for people with a lot of money to be happy because they're always worrying about their money or thinking about making more money. Lots of times rich people are actually *unhappy* because they believe the false idea that money is supposed to make them happy, but deep down they know it doesn't.

Bottom line: Don't waste your time thinking or dreaming about how much money you'll make some- day.

33. SOME PEOPLE HATE THEIR JOBS—CAN I FIND ONE I LIKE?

In a word—ABSOLUTELY!

Some people believe work is a curse. But God designed us to be productive—and to enjoy accomplishing stuff. Look what the Bible says in Ecclesiastes 3:22: "So I saw that there is nothing better for people than to enjoy their work."

So *why* do so many people really hate their jobs? Well, let's look at this from a different angle. We'll give you some reasons why people hate their jobs—and then you can do the opposite.

To get a job you hate:

1. CHOOSE A CAREER TOTALLY BASED ON SOMEONE ELSE'S OPINION.

When you pick a job, you're definitely smart to listen to the thoughts of people who know you well. But if you want to hate your job, then let someone else pick your career path—even if you know it doesn't fit who you are. Like, maybe your mom wants you to become a lawyer, or perhaps your uncle hopes and dreams that you'll take over the family business. Both of those ideas make you want to throw up. But you can choose to do one of them anyway—and vomit your way into the workforce.

2. MAKE DECISIONS COMPLETELY BASED ON MONEY.

The last chapter talks about how much money is "enough." If you want to hate your job, then consider only the size of the paycheck. Then even if you're miserable all week long, at least you'll be able to wear fancy clothes while you hate your job.

3. DON'T EVER TRY ANYTHING NEW.
Pick a career and stick with it—no matter what. If you sense there's another job that might fit you better, just be too afraid to check it out. You can also be stubborn and say stuff like, "At least I'm getting a paycheck," or "It's too risky to explore something that I might like better."

Okay, let's be clear: Those three suggestions *don't make any sense.* But too many people use these strategies in their searches for jobs, and they end up feeling miserable when they don't have to. We (Marko and Scott) *love* our jobs. Even though they aren't perfect, and they're even frustrating at times, our jobs are great for who God wired each of us to be.

Do you know anyone who really *loves* her job? A teacher? A parent? An aunt? Ask her why she loves it so much and what it took for her to get to that place. And remember, Ecclesiastes 3:22 can be true for you, too.

34. MY FIRST BOSS—YIKES!

You might not have your first job until you're in high school or beyond. And that's totally fine (in some ways, it's great). But many (most?) middle schoolers end up having some kind of paying job during their young teenage years. It might not be a regular job, but most will start babysitting children or mowing lawns or doing something for which they get paid. Those do count as jobs!

Your work may not seem like a "real job" yet. But if you're getting paid, then you most likely have a boss. And the boss, of course, is the person you're responsible to, the person who chose to hire you (the person who's paying you). If you're babysitting, then the kids' mom or dad is your boss. If you're mowing a lawn, then the person who asked you to mow is your boss.

Throughout your life you'll find there are good bosses and bad bosses. Good bosses pay you fairly, treat you with respect, understand that you have a life outside of the job, and have reasonable and clearly defined expectations for you. Bad bosses do the opposite: They might pay you unfairly, treat you with disrespect, demand that you live for your job, or have unreasonable expectations about what you can actually do during your time on the job. It's been our experience that a good boss plays a bigger role in your liking the job than how much money you earn.

Here are a few tips for how to get along with a boss:

• BE ON TIME.

This is a HUGE deal to every boss in the universe. Seriously. If you don't show up when you say you'll show up, then your boss will assume you can't be trusted with other stuff.

• SPEAKING OF TRUST: BE WORTHY OF IT.

Be honest. Don't be sneaky. Say what you can do and then make sure you do it. These actions will build your boss's trust, and he'll want to give you more responsibility. (Check out the Parable of the Talents for an example of this. It's found in Matthew 25:14-28.)

• TREAT YOUR BOSS WITH RESPECT.

Sometimes this is easy to do—like when you like your boss. But this one can be really tough to do if your boss is a grouch or isn't nice to you. Either way, it's important to show respect to the person who employs you. If you cannot find a way to respect your boss, then you need to find another job.

SECTION 7

PARENT RELATIONSHIPS

35. A CHANGING RELATIONSHIP: PARENTS BECOMING "COACHES"

Did you play T-ball when you were a little kid? If so, you remember the coach first *told* you how to hit a T-ball—then *showed* you how to hit a T-ball. And finally the coach gave you a chance to try it yourself. (Did you ever swing the bat, hit only air, and fall down? Yeah, me, too.)

In baseball a coach starts by putting a ball on a tee, then throws some pitches to a player, and eventually shows the player how to pitch to a batter. Ultimately, a coach can't play baseball *for* you, but a coach can help you learn how to play. Well, in the game known as "your life," your parents are basically trying to use that same teaching process with you. And when it works the way it's supposed to, the role of a parent is a pretty cool thing. Really!

When you're born, you need someone to do *everything* for you, right? Parents feed you, burp you, and change your smelly diapers. But the goal of a parent is never to *keep* doing all that stuff for you. (Good thing, cuz it'd be pretty awkward to have your mom or dad grabbing the TP for you, now wouldn't it?)

The role of a parent is supposed to *change* over time. Somebody smart once said that parenting is the only relationship in which the ultimate goal is separation. That's because parents are supposed to train their children so one day they can move out and live on their own. And it's not unusual for teenagers to start feeling a desire to pull away from their parents during the middle school years.

Even though parents can sometimes be annoying and embarrassing, remember that they were also in middle school once. It can actually be very valuable to lean into the coaching they give you. Even professional athletes who play at the highest possible level have coaches to help them continue to play better. Their coaches almost always used to play the sport and still recognize how to do it well. Some athletes pay attention to their coaches and improve. Others are puffed up and overconfident and often lose out because they think they're too good for coaching.

As your parents move into this new coaching role with you, here are a couple of tips for you:

1. BE COACHABLE.
Allow your parents to give you advice, partially cuz it can help you deal with the stuff you won't expect.

2. ASK YOUR COACHES GOOD QUESTIONS.
"*Why* should I do it that way?" "What can I learn from this?" "How did you mess up when you were my age?"

Pay attention to your parent-coaches—because surviving middle school is way more important than learning how to play T-ball.

HUMANS CAN DETECT A SKUNK'S SMELL A MILE AWAY.

36. CURFEW: WHAT'S FAIR?
(NOW AND IN THE FUTURE)

Curfew (the time when you have to be home at night) is a whole new thing to most middle school students. When you were, like, five years old, you never had a conversation like this with your parents:

You: Mommy and Daddy?

Parents: Yes, honey?

You: What time do I have to be home tonight?

Parents: What are your plans, little one?

You: My homies and I are gonna wander the neighborhood and see what kind of trouble we can get into.

Parents: Uh, then you need to be home by 6 p.m.

Nope. That conversation never happened. The big issue back then was more likely your bedtime. And lots of middle school kids still have bedtimes. (It's actually a great thing to have a bedtime, by the way—and the earlier the better. Sleep helps your brain grow.)

Your bedtime will become less of an issue between you and your parents during these next few years, while your curfew will become a bigger issue. Most teenagers and parents really struggle over curfews because teenagers always want their curfews to be later, and parents usually think nothing good can happen after a certain time at night.

We can't tell you the perfect curfew time. (It changes with your age and other issues.) But we can give you some advice on how to increase your chances of having a curfew you can live with:

• DON'T FIGHT ABOUT IT ALL THE TIME

Parents get massively bugged when their teenagers fight about the same subjects over and over. It's okay to bring it up and have a calm discussion. But if you allow the conversation to get emotional or if you raise your voice or if you say whiny things like, "You treat me like a baby!" then your parents will be *less likely* to give you a curfew that'll make you happy.

• DON'T BREAK CURFEW.

That means don't come home later than you agreed to do. Seriously, the very best path to a curfew you want is proving you'll be responsible with whatever curfew you have. Getting home on time also shows your parents you respect their decisions, which will help them trust you more—and perhaps give you a later curfew...sooner!

• COMMUNICATE

Tell your parents where you are and when you'll be home—even if you'll be home before your curfew. Your parents are concerned about your safety. Giving them a quick call to make sure they know where you are will build their trust, too. Also, when you're about to head home, call them to say you're on the way. (One more big-time tip: If, for some really unfortunate reason you just can't make it home by curfew—like your friend's parent's car got a flat tire—then it's super-massively important that you call and let your folks know what's up.

37. HOW TO ARGUE BETTER

Okay—we're going to offer you a little insider tip here: We (Marko and Scott) are both parents of middle schoolers, so this is kind of like getting top-secret information from the other side.

First, when we say "the other side," that's not exactly right. Try not to think of your parents as the enemies. For example, if your goal is to win an argument with your folks, but you tick 'em off in the process, then you haven't really won anything.

But it's not really about winning and losing anyway—it's about growing up. So here's some stuff that *won't work* when you and your parents disagree—and some stuff that *will*. Usually.

WON'T WORK

• LOSING YOUR COOL
If you yell, stomp your feet, call your parents "stupid," or roll your eyes and make that awesome groaning noise, then you're probably guaranteed a bad outcome.

• INTERRUPTING
You like to be listened to, right? Well, so do your parents. Even if they say something that's incorrect, you should wait until they've finished speaking before you (appropriately) tell them how you see it differently.

• TALKING DOWN TO YOUR PARENT
Nobody likes to be treated like an idiot. Hold back the "attitude" even when you want to unload.

CAN WORK

• BE RESPECTFUL THE *WHOLE* TIME.

I (Marko) used to get *so* mad at my parents, especially when I felt like they weren't hearing me. But when I was disrespectful to them, it always tanked the conversation.

• CALL A "TIME-OUT."

This isn't the kind of time-out a toddler gets for smearing applesauce on the dog. This is asking for a five-minute pause so you can get your thoughts together. When you feel like you're about to lose your cool, say something like, "Can we take a five-minute break so I can think?" But be sure to come back to the discussion.

• LISTEN TO "THE OTHER SIDE" AND CALMLY EXPLAIN HOW YOU SEE IT.

Ask good questions and try to see things from your parents' viewpoint so you can show them how you see it differently. If you don't understand their point, then you won't know what you're arguing against.

When our *own* kids argue with us this way, they stand a way better chance of getting what they want.

Parents aren't always right; but when an argument turns into a good discussion, everybody can win. Usually.

"MY PARENTS ARE ANNOYING SOMETIMES—AND EMBARRASSING."
—JAYNA, 8TH GRADE

A DELTIOLOGIST IS SOMEONE WHO COLLECTS POSTCARDS.

38. UNDERSTANDING MY PARENTS' "PROBLEMS"

Lots of middle schoolers—probably going back to dinosaur times—have said, "My parents just don't understand me." But, believe it or not, many parents think, *My kids just don't understand me!*

Understanding is the key word in this chapter title because it's not up to you to fix, solve, or rescue your parents from their problems. You should focus on your own middle school problems for right now. But just by considering and appreciating the fact that you're not the only one facing problems and challenges—well, that'll go a long way in helping your relationship with your parents.

Middle school is challenging partly because you've never done it before, right? Well, think about this: Your parents have never *parented* a middle schooler like you before, either. Even if you have an older brother or sister, you're a different person. So every kid presents new challenges for the parents. If your mom or dad or your stepmom or stepdad seem to be struggling with the parenting thing, then maybe it's cuz they're figuring out how to *parent* a teenager at the same time you're figuring out how to *be* one.

Besides the huge mission of parenting well, your folks have lots of other pressures, too. Career challenges are big for most parents. (God created work to be good—but every job has its difficulties.) Money challenges are always tricky, and they also help explain why parents say annoying stuff like,

"Close that door! Do you think we're trying to heat the whole neighborhood?" Almost all parents have marriage challenges, too—how to be a good husband or wife, or how to be a good ex-husband or ex-wife. Add to the pile any other issues with their health, extended family, neighbors, and so on—and it all sounds pretty challenging, doesn't it?

Here are three suggestions to help you build a better relationship with your parents:

• PRAY FOR 'EM.

You don't know what it's like to be a parent—but God does. And God can help you understand your parents. Ask God!

• BE PATIENT WITH 'EM.

Even though they're old (don't tell them we said that), your parents are still learning. Take a deep breath and cut 'em a little slack.

• TELL YOUR PARENTS YOU'RE PROUD OF 'EM WHEN THEY DO SOMETHING REALLY COOL.

It feels good when someone tells you that you got something right, doesn't it? Most kids forget their parents like to hear this kind of praise, too.

If you do these things, we bet your parents will tell someone what an encouragement you are to them—and they just might feel like you understand them better.

39. HONORING MY PARENTS

We're sure you've heard this verse. (I mean, even kids who've never seen a Bible have heard it):

Honor your father and your mother...

The verse is Exodus 20:12. While the idea of honoring your parents is found throughout the Bible, this verse is the most famous—and for a very good reason: It's one of the Ten Commandments. That's right. God gave Moses and the Israelites 10 big rules for living, and this is one of them. God felt this command was important enough to include in the same list as "Don't kill people" and "Don't steal stuff." In fact—are you ready for this?—"Honor your father and your mother" is listed *before* those other two!

What does it mean to "honor" someone? It means to give respect and to treat a person well. Why is that such a big deal to God? Well, there are probably a bunch of reasons, including these:

- God gave the responsibility for your care, maturity, and spiritual growth to your parents.

- God knows the whole family system works better if you honor your parents so they don't always have to discipline you or fight with you to get you to obey their rules.

- God wants us to honor him, and honoring our parents helps us learn how to honor God.

But we want to give you another reason—one from a totally different angle:

- Honoring your parents is best for *you*. God wants you to honor your parents because God loves you and wants you to have the best life ever. And God knows—because God created the whole world—that honoring your parents is a big part of your having the best life possible.

How does honoring your parents help you have a better life? Here are a couple of ideas:

- Teenagers who honor their parents are happier and more content. We've seen it over and over again. There are lots of reasons for this—but it's really just that simple.

- Honoring your parents decreases your chances of getting hurt. Let's face it: Parents have more wisdom and life experience than you do. They don't *always* know what's better for you, but they *usually* do.

So treat your parents with respect and try to do what they ask you to do. Seriously, it will make your life better.

40. LEAVING HOME, MOVING AWAY

At this point in your life, the idea of one day moving away and living on your own probably brings up one of two responses:

- No way! I can't imagine leaving home.

- I can't wait! That would be so amazing!

Moving out on your own is a future reality (at least for most people). We (Marko and Scott) have noticed three different situations when young adults tend to move out of their parents' homes:

- A bunch do it because they go away to college—somewhere that's not within driving distance of home. And they'll usually live in a dorm with other college students.

- A second group may or may not go to college, but they move out as quickly as possible after high school graduation, usually sharing a super-cheap dump of an apartment with a couple of friends.

- And the third group—which is becoming more common—waits to move out (whether or not they go to college) until they're in their late 20s.

Each situation has its own challenges:

- Those who move into college dorms live in extremely crowded conditions and often with roommates they didn't choose. Plus, college dorms (especially at non-Christian colleges) are full of every kind of temptation that's just waiting to mess up your life.

- Those who move out quickly usually struggle to pay the bills. They also live in a place that's not exactly a dream come true because it's all they can afford.

- Those who wait before moving out have it the easiest in many ways. But they often experience more conflict with their parents over rules and expectations. After all, these 20-somethings are adults, but they're still living under their parents' roofs. And sometimes they have to live with some teasing from their friends—"Oh, you still live with your mommy and daddy?"

Moving out on your own is a part of growing up, and in many ways it's one of the BIGGIES. In our culture you're considered an adult when you can take complete responsibility for yourself. So really, when you're (someday) trying to decide if it's time to move out, the big question to ask yourself is: Am I ready to take full responsibility for myself?

I WAS A MIDDLE SCHOOL DORK!
—SCOTT

I was a dork in a lot of the day-to-day moments of middle school.

- I had my own paper route when I was in middle school. These days, most newspapers are delivered by adults driving cars. But back then, I rode my bike from house to house, launching papers onto about 70 or 80 front porches every single day. I got pretty good at heaving them from my bike while I rode no-handed. But about once a week, I'd land one on somebody's roof. More than a few went right through people's windows, too.

The worst part of having a paper route was collecting the money. Now you'd think that part would be kinda cool. And for the first 50 or 60 people, it was. But getting the last 10 or 12 payments was always a hassle. Those customers would never seem to be home, or they always had some great reason why they couldn't cough up $6.40. So nearly every month my mom would get on my case about finishing my collections from the last few holdouts. And nearly every month I'd tell her I was going to do it and would even leave the house as I said it. But then I'd ride my bike to the Silver Castle Video Arcade and pump quarters into the old-school video games instead. I can't imagine how much money I just never collected!

- I got pretty good grades in school, but even that accomplishment earned me some dork moments. In sixth-grade math, we all had to take some standardized test. Fine, no sweat. But when the results came back, I'd "won" one of the top three spots for my school. I'd heard of passing a test before, but I'd never heard of winning one! So I thought it was kinda cool...until I found out what the prize was. The winners got to go downtown and take another test. And this time we were competing against students from all over the city. And the test was on a Saturday, no less! What kind of a prize was that? "You win—another test!" Come on!

I'm actually surprised I survived middle school math. My teacher was a really tall and skinny guy, and he used to walk around the classroom while he taught us. Sometimes he'd gently thump students on their heads with his gigantic ring. It was so annoying. But he seemed to really amuse himself by doing it. Nobody liked it, but everybody was too afraid to say anything to him—maybe because it seemed like his head was way up near the ceiling. Finally, he'd thumped me one too many times, and I sort of growled at him, "Cut it out, shorty!" Another trip to the principal's office for me.

- One of my best buddies in middle school was a guy we called "Bubba" because he was tall and strong. He also had this condition where his feet would blister so bad that he had to use a wheelchair at school. So I'd push him down the hallway as fast as I could and then let go to see if he could stop the wheelchair before it hit something. I don't know why I did this. He was my friend, after all. But it seemed cool at the time. I'd also sometimes ram his chair into whatever girl he had a crush on. Real nice, huh? Bubba and I are still friends today...and he still thinks I'm kind of a dork!

FRIEND RELATIONSHIPS

41. HOW FRIENDSHIPS "MORPH" OVER TIME

Morph is just a fancy word for "change." One thing you can be sure of in middle school is that things do change, right? You change from elementary school to middle school, your appearance changes (you get taller), and your voice (if you're a boy) starts to change. In fact, if there were one word that best describes the middle school years, it'd be *change*.

So it kinda makes sense that we should also expect our *friendships* to change. In a lot of ways, change is good. (If the two of us hadn't changed any since middle school, then we'd be pretty funny-looking dads!) But as your interests grow and change, it really *can* affect your friendships—and this "morphing" has the potential to be challenging at times.

Have you ever watched little kids on a playground? Every child I know likes slides and sandboxes. So even two young children who just met can become great "friends" in a short amount of time. Maybe you've got a friendship that started on a playground back in elementary school. But as time has passed, you've become more interested in computers, while your friend is more interested in sports or cheerleading. Or one of you is becoming more interested in dating, while the other one doesn't see what the big deal is. Or whatever—something has changed.

When it comes to long-term friendships hitting the middle school years, you should *expect* that things will change, just as your interests do. That's normal.

Almost every day in elementary school, 1 (Scott) played street baseball with the two brothers who lived in the house next door to me—Todd and Steven. But as the years went on, 1 spent more time with my buddies on the swim team, while Todd played basketball and Steven played golf. We were still friends (check out the next chapter)—but our friendship definitely morphed.

We're *not* saying that *all* your friendships will change, but the ones that don't will probably be the exceptions. If you're feeling pressure to be "into" something that your long-time friend enjoys or to keep the friendship the way it's always been—then depressurize yourself.

Morphing can actually be pretty cool!

42. LEAVING SOME OLD FRIENDSHIPS AND STARTING SOME NEW ONES

In the last chapter we talked about how friendships morph and change. When they do, there may come a time to leave behind some old friendships.

How do you do that?

Well, even if you're moving from having a really close friendship to having a relationship that's a little more distant, you don't want to bail on that person completely. Romans 12:16 says, "Live in harmony with one another." (BTW, this is true even if the person *isn't* your closest friend.)

Have you ever heard people sing a song off-key? It makes you cringe. But when the harmony is right, then the music just flows—it feels natural. So when you feel like you're moving away from some of your older friendships, think about harmony and try a couple of things, like:

1. ASK YOURSELF, *AM I LEAVING THIS FRIENDSHIP TOO EARLY?*

Maybe you're not on the same team or in the same club with this person, but you still see your relationship with her as valuable. If the friendship's still valuable to you, then think of some ways you can stay connected to the person when it doesn't happen as naturally as it used to. On the bus, online, in-between classes—even short connections can keep good friendships going.

2. IF A FRIENDSHIP SEEMS DESTINED FOR MORE DISTANCE, TRY TO MAKE SURE THERE'S STILL "FRIENDLINESS" IN THE RELATIONSHIP.

Bailing out on a friendship because you're ticked at somebody isn't cool. Do your best to make peace and keep the "harmony" in every relationship, not just your closest ones.

When you're looking for newer friendships, an obvious place to search is among people who have something in common with you. Those connections will probably be easy to make. But don't just look in the obvious places. As you get older, some of your most exciting friendships can be with people who are different from you—at least at first glance. If you skip out on potential friendships because you think someone's "too different" from you, then you might miss out on something great.

Why not make a list right now—right here on this page—of other middle schoolers you "sorta" know who might be great "future friends"? In a couple of years, you could look back at this list and see the name of a now-great friend.

"WHY DO PEOPLE WANT TO BE FRIENDS ONE DAY, BUT NOT THE NEXT?"
—JEN, 7TH GRADE

43. ROOMMATES: WHAT'LL *THAT* BE LIKE?

For some of you, the idea of having a roommate is like, "So? I share a room now. What's the big deal?" But for others who've had their own spaces for most of their lives, the idea of having a roommate someday (either in college or in your first apartment) is a whole new idea.

I (Marko) had never shared a bedroom before I went away to college. Growing up, I had two older sisters, and my room was in the basement (lots of privacy!). But in my freshman year at a Christian college, I got my first roommate. His name was Nick, and—other than the fact that we're both Christians—we had absolutely nothing in common. He was into classical music, and he played in the orchestra. I was into punk music. Nick went to bed early, and he got up early. I stayed up late, and I slept late. He studied hard (pre-med), and he was serious about school. I didn't study much, and I was a lousy student. So it shouldn't surprise you that we had some conflict. Yup—we had lots of it.

Most of our conflicts were the quiet, murmuring kind. (Nick would mumble something under his breath about my music; I'd throw a pillow at him when he was making noise early in the morning.) But a couple of times our quiet conflicts turned not so quiet. And then there was the messiness of figuring out how to live together—in a room the size of a closet—after we'd had a fight.

Even a roommate who's a great friend can create issues and conflict. But there are two major keys to keeping your sanity when you have a roommate (and this will also serve as good advice for those of you who share a room now):

COMMUNICATE.

It's essential that you know what's important to your roommate. Nick *did not* want me to touch his books or anything on his desk. Okay, that was fine with me once I understood it. I *did not* want Nick to be noisy early in the morning. He slowly figured this out and got better at it. If you show some respect for the things that are important to your roommate, then things between you will go more smoothly. This also means you have to communicate what's important to you. (People can't read your mind.)

COMPROMISE.

There will be times when your desires and the desires of your roommate will conflict. It's pretty much unavoidable. This usually means you have to find a solution in the middle—something that works for both of you, even if it isn't exactly what either person wants. For example, Nick and I agreed that anytime we were both in the room, we would alternate every hour who could choose the music.

GOD/CHURCH RELATIONSHIP

44. STAYING CONNECTED TO GOD

If you've grown up in a church, then you've probably heard a lot of Bible stories. Moses parted the Red Sea. Noah brought a whole bunch of animals onto the ark. Jonah was swallowed by a great fish which later vomited him back on to dry land.

Little kids trust. Parents could probably tell their tots there's a giant, invisible gorilla named Tim who protects their house from robbers and other dangers, and their kids would believe it...for a while. But as they get older—not so much.

Questions will come up, but that's not a bad thing. *Actually*, it's really good! We (Marko and Scott) LOVE your questions cuz leaning into those questions—asking them and trying to figuring out the answers—is one of the best ways we've found to get to know God better and stay connected to him. Even when the questions seem hard. If you just try to "have more faith" without getting the answers to your questions, there's no doubt that distance will grow between you and God.

Do you want to get the *most* out of your questions? Check out these tips:

QUESTION WITH HONESTY.

God isn't afraid of your questions. God's *not* sitting on a throne, listening to your questions, and then angrily thundering, "Have faith, not questions!" God knows that asking questions is a great way to develop a deeper faith. And God says, "Bring it on!" because God's ready and waiting.

QUESTION WITH OWNERSHIP.

When you wonder about something—own it! Accept the challenge of looking for the answer—first in the Bible (which is why God gave it to us), and then ask a parent, friend, or youth pastor who knows where to search. If you wait for someone to knock on your door and say, "Here's your answer!" then you'll be waiting...and waiting...and waiting...and waiting... You get the idea, right?

QUESTION WITH OTHERS.

Got a small group of friends at church? Know anyone else who really wants to stay connected with God (or maybe *get* connected with God)? When you've got people who will talk through your questions with you, you can find the answers together.

So don't just be quiet and try to have more faith. Start asking questions! (Especially if you believe that Tim the Gorilla is protecting your house.)

45. WHY DO SOME KIDS "FADE AWAY" FROM GOD AND THE CHURCH?

Maybe you've noticed that some of the kids who were an active part of your church in elementary school just aren't around anymore. Or you may have a friend who had a real relationship with Jesus once but she just doesn't seem to care about God now. If you haven't noticed this kind of thing yet, then you probably will in the next few years.

It's really common for teenagers—especially older teenagers and young adults—to "fade away" from God and the church. But just because it's common, that doesn't mean it's an okay thing. Just the opposite—it's a big bummer!

There are a few reasons why this "fade" happens:

TEENAGERS GO THROUGH LOTS OF CHANGES— THEIR FAITH MUST ALSO CHANGE.

(If you haven't already, you should check out *My Changes*, the fifth book in the Middle School Survival Series, to learn more about this.) Because your brain and how you think is changing like crazy, your faith also needs to change. You now have the ability to think about God and faith stuff in a whole new (more adult) way. So it's massively important that you wrestle with what you believe and allow your faith to grow and change—in other words, become more of an adult faith than a little-kid faith. The problem is that some teenagers *never* wrestle with their faith. They coast into and through their teenage years with the same faith and beliefs they had when they were little kids. But in reality, an eight-year-old's faith doesn't answer all of the questions or address all of the issues that a 17-year-old must face. So many teenagers fade away from God because they're going through life with a faith that doesn't make sense anymore.

LOTS OF CHURCHES SPEND MORE TIME TALKING ABOUT HOW TO "BE A GOOD KID" THAN HOW TO HAVE A REAL RELATIONSHIP WITH GOD.

That stuff gets pretty old by the time you're in middle school and high school. If teenagers don't have a faith that helps them connect with the real God who loves them and knows them, then it's just a list of do's and don'ts.

THERE ARE *SO* MANY TEMPTATIONS FOR OLDER TEENAGERS.

(And this is true for many young teenagers, too.) Lots of teenagers chuck their faith because they believe these other things will make them happier than a relationship with God.

46. IF YOU COULD "PICK YOUR OWN CHURCH"...

Some of you have already chosen a church. Maybe some of you have parents who don't go to church. Or maybe your parents do go to a church, but you attend a different church with a friend. If so, then you already have some experience with this idea. But most middle schoolers go to church with their parents and didn't help choose the church.

Sooner or later, most Christians have an opportunity to choose a church. You might never move more than a few miles away from home (even if you move out of your parents' house someday); therefore, it's possible that you will always attend the same church you do now. But even then, you'll be *making the choice* to stay at that church.

But if you do move to a different city (or to a different part of the same city), then you'll probably have to choose a new church to attend. A few tips:

• DON'T BLOW IT OFF.

We've seen so many young adults (and older adults) who just stopped going to church after they moved or when they felt they needed to move on from their church for a different reason. Finding a new church can be awkward—you don't know the people there, you don't know what's normal, you don't know the regular schedule. And since church is supposed to be a community (a group of people that knows and cares about each other), it's tough to "try" other churches where you aren't a part of the community yet.

• JUMP IN AND TRY A BUNCH OF CHURCHES.

Trying new churches gives us a great opportunity to stretch our faith. So make a schedule and try a different church each week for a month or two. Think about what you believe (because churches have lots of different beliefs) and do a little research to see if the beliefs of the churches you visit line up with what you believe about God, the Bible, and what the Christian life looks like. Even if you try a church that's a part of the same denomination as your parents' church, you might find it's *very* different from your home church.

• LAND SOMEWHERE.

Don't be a long-term "church shopper." It's really important to plant yourself and get involved in the community of a local church. So find a place that feels like a good fit and give it a long try (that includes getting involved with a ministry there). After a year or so, you might find it's not the best fit for you. But you'll never know if it *is* the right fit if you attend only once in a while and never dive in.

47. YOUR INVOLVEMENT: *BEING* THE CHURCH INSTEAD OF JUST ATTENDING

Lots of people believe church is just somewhere you go. In reality, church is something you be. (Okay, your English teacher would say, "Something you *are*." But "be" sounds better.)

You've probably heard something like this before: "If your church building burns down, is the *church* gone?" The answer: No way! The church isn't a building—the church is the people in that building. Everyone who believes in Jesus is part of the church.

As you hit the middle school years, you'll have more chances to BE church! And there are two main places where this can happen:

IN THE CHURCH BUILDING

How can you contribute to what's going on in your church by doing something you love to do? God has gifted everyone with contributions they can make to their churches. Helping teach and take care of little kids, doing music, welcoming new people, or helping old people—the list is endless. What do you love to do? Think about a way you could do that to help the church.

EVERYWHERE ELSE!

Did you know that the best "advertisement" for God is people who call themselves Christians? Did you also know that the *worst advertisement* for God is people who call themselves Christians but don't live like Jesus (although they might act like him while they're *in* the church building)? Every time you love someone, care for someone, or show concern for someone; every time you defend the person who's least, or lost, or last—*that's* when you're being the church.

You don't need to hand someone a business card that says, I JUST HELPED YOU BECAUSE I GO TO _____ (NAME OF YOUR CHURCH). (In fact, don't do that—you'd look like a dork!) But as you care about the people around you, you *are* the church! Or you BE the church (if you're not in English class, that is).

Pretty cool.

48. CREDIT CARDS: FREE MONEY!

Do you remember the first time you watched an adult whip out a little piece of plastic at the store? It seemed like with one little "swipe," she could walk out of there with *whatever* she wanted! *Ridiculously cool!* is the phrase that came to our minds, and we bet you thought something similar. You probably also thought that if you could just get your hands on one of those, you'd be all set, right? Snacks, movies, music, pets, iPods, iPhones, other iStuff—there's *nothing* you couldn't buy with that plastic.

That's where the problems start. You see, when you use a credit card, you're basically making a promise to pay the money back someday. And that little "swiper box" communicates directly with the credit card company so it can keep track of EVERY penny you owe.

Within a month, you'll be asked to pay it all back. But if you don't (or can't) pay back the *entire* amount within those 30 days, then your credit card company will charge you an extra fee (finance charge). It's called "interest," and the percentage rate of that interest is usually very high. So before you know it, you can end up owing a lot, *lot*, LOT (did I mention that it's a LOT?) more money than you initially spent.

Did you know that the *average* family in America owes $8,000 in credit-card debt? Statistics say that *most* people don't pay off the whole amount that's due on their credit cards each month, which means they'll owe *more* money the next month—even if they never buy another thing with their cards. That's because the credit card companies add on that "finance charge" (or the amount of interest owed) every month.

Proverbs 22:7 says, "The borrower is slave to the lender." (Think of the "borrower" as someone with an unpaid credit card bill.) Using a credit card is like spending money you don't have—and that's just dangerous, cuz somebody in a bank somewhere is gonna want that money back. And until you pay back all you owe, you won't truly be "free."

When you spend cash (dollar bills and coins), there's an "emotion" attached to it, isn't there? When you count out those dollars to buy your movie ticket, you can kind of *feel* it. And that's good! But when you plunk down a piece of plastic, you don't experience that same level of emotion. It's more like the magical "get in free" card, except using it can actually make the experience more expensive (and painful) than you've ever imagined.

After you graduate from high school, credit card companies will invite you to get your own "plastic magic." But college students often spend like crazy and then end up owing money until they're 30 years old and beyond. It's ridiculously *un*cool.

You probably don't have credit card offers coming your way just yet. But when you do—be wise. Talk to someone you trust about how to handle your money. And don't get sucked in by the free-money lie.

"CREDIT CARDS SOUND FUN. BUT TO AVOID OVERSPENDING, I THINK I'LL STICK WITH CASH."

—TANNER, 6TH GRADE

49. SAVING

We're fairly sure you've heard—from your parents, a teacher, or even on TV—that it's smart to save your money. But let's be honest: It's a lot more fun to *spend* money than it is to *save* it. And we can speak from both perspectives here because Scott is pretty good at saving money, and Marko is lousy at it.

Maybe your parents make you save a portion of everything you earn. It might bug you to have to do this, but it's really a great habit to have.

WHY IS IT SMART TO SAVE YOUR MONEY?

There are two main reasons:

TO PREPARE FOR THE UNEXPECTED

Saving your money can help you when a surprise comes up that requires a bunch of money. Take Marko's two kids, for example. Marko's son is great at saving; when he wants to consider buying something (for himself or someone else) or giving a chunk of his money away, he's able to do so. When he was eight, he'd saved enough money to buy himself a $200 bird! But Marko's daughter—although she has a ton of other amazing qualities—isn't very good at saving. She spends what she has, which means she never has any money.

TO SPARE YOU FROM EXTRA STRESS

Saving money can make you less stressed (especially when you're an adult with lots of bills to pay) because you're not just living from paycheck to paycheck.

HOW CAN YOU SAVE MONEY?

Some people seem to be wired to save. They sock away their money in a bank or a box, and they're super cautious about buying stuff. But for others (like Marko!), saving money takes discipline—it has to be a choice. That means you have to decide *before* you get the money— and, for sure, *before* you want to buy something—that you're going to put aside a certain amount of all the money you receive (as a gift, or as pay, or from an allowance). If you take one-fourth of all the money you receive and put it in a place that isn't easy to get to (like a bank account), then you'll be amazed at how quickly it becomes a big chunk o' change.

Not everyone in America has the option to save. Some people just don't make enough money to set some aside each month. But *most people* can save a portion of their money—if they choose to.

Oh, and just because a sign or a store advertisement says you can "save money" by shopping there, remember: If you're buying something, then you're still *spending* money, not saving it.

50. WHAT ABOUT TITHING?

Let's get the pronunciation lesson out of the way. When we first saw the word *tithing*, we thought it should sound like "teething." But that's what babies do whenever they get new teeth. Then we thought it rhymed with "with-ing," you know, like "tith-ing." But that's not it, either.

Here's the right way to say it: It sounds like TY-thing. (Not a Marko-thing. Not a Scott-thing. A Ty-thing. Got it? Good!)

On to the next question: Have you ever wondered why you don't have to buy a ticket to go to church? (Some of you may be thinking, *Have you ever* been *to my church? No one would ever pay to go there!*)

Seriously, though, think about it: How can a church keep running weekly services, hosting youth events, giving money to people in need, and doing the zillion other things that churches do? Well, that's where the tithing comes in.

The word *tithe* actually means "one-tenth." Malachi 3:10 says, "Bring the whole tithe into the storehouse, that there may be food in my house." God is telling each of us that a tenth of what we earn—our income—should automatically go back to God's work.

That sounds pretty difficult, especially since one of the first words that all babies learn to say is *mine*. Maybe you have a little brother or sister, or maybe you've watched this scene play out in the church nursery: A toddler grabs a toy and says, "MINE!" It doesn't matter if the toy really belongs to that child or not. It's just the kid's way of saying, "I like stuff, and I'm claiming this as my own." It cracks me up when a baby grabs something like an iPod or a cell phone and says, "Mine!" *Right. Like you'd even know what to do with it, little baby.*

The best word to describe the stuff in your life isn't *mine*; it's *God's*. After all, who made it possible for you to have all the stuff you have? In Acts 4:32 it says, "No one claimed that any of their possessions was their own, but they shared everything they had." And that church was like *magical*—God poured out blessings upon them (see Acts 4:33-35). In the same way, we can trust that God will continue to provide for our needs when we give a portion of our money back to the church.

So when you start making money of your own, *look forward* to tithing—giving 10 percent or more—to your church. It all belongs to God anyway, right?

"IT'S A GOOD RESPONSIBILITY BECAUSE YOU'RE GIVING [SOMETHING] BACK TO GOD [AND THANKING HIM] FOR WHAT HE'S GIVEN [TO] YOU."

—JEREMY, 7TH GRADE

MARRIAGE

51. IS THERE "ONE RIGHT PERSON" FOR ME?

Awww! What a romantic question. If this is one of the first chapters you chose to read, then we bet you like the love story, chick-flick style movies, huh? *My Prince Charming Awaits*, or maybe it's *My Princess Charming*.

Speaking of movies, "finding the right one" is a common theme on the big screen. Did you ever wonder why? Well, it's partly because humans are *designed* for relationship. Guess that's why most people are suckers for a good love story. God hardwired each of us with the desire for relationship.

When God made the first man (see Genesis chapter 2) God said, "It is not good for the man to be alone" (Genesis 2:18). Up 'til that point, God had declared everything else he'd made "good." But seeing Adam all by himself made God shake his head and say, "Nope."

So back to the question at the top of the page: Is there a "right one" for you? Well, we've given this a lot of thought. And yes, in fact, there is a Right One for you.

It's...God!

Wait, wait, wait...we're not just giving you the churchy answer. We promise! But when you're thinking about whether there's a right "romantic match" for you, you need to start with God. But some of us get so caught up in thinking and worrying about whether there's a perfect match for us—we forget to trust God to provide it.

Look at Luke 12, starting with verse 22:

> Then Jesus said to his disciples: "Therefore I tell you, do not worry about your life…Who of you by worrying can add a single hour to your life? Since you cannot do this very little thing, why do you worry about the rest?" (vv. 22, 25-26)

God does care about your life—from the big stuff on down to the littlest details. And God is the only one who knows the future. So are you willing to trust God with the romantic angle of the movie called *Your Life?*

God's not going to leave you alone in it. If you stick close to God and don't go overboard worrying about it, then who knows? Maybe Hollywood will make a movie about you and your "right one" someday.

"MARRIAGE IS GOOD BECAUSE YOU CAN WAKE UP EVERY MORNING KNOWING YOU ARE LOVED."

—CAROLINE, 8TH GRADE

52. SHOULD I EVEN BE THINKING ABOUT THIS NOW?

Hmmm...? This is a great question. Our super-sure, totally definite, completely honest, and final answer is "no and yes." That clears it up, huh?

That's it—we don't have any more to say about this.

We're just kidding. (We do that. We're kidders.)

Okay, so NO, you shouldn't bother thinking about marriage yet. C'mon, you're just 12 or 13 years old, or maybe you're 14 or 11. Marriage, if it ever becomes a reality for you, is a LONG way off. Enjoy being a middle schooler. The time to start thinking about marriage will come—in 10 or 20 years.

But then YES, you *should* start thinking about it. We don't mean you should start looking for someone to marry (duh!) or shopping for wedding rings. But here are a couple of things you might start doing in preparation for a possible marriage someday:

START A QUALITIES HUNT.

Huh? What we mean is you should start taking notice of the personal qualities you'd want in the person you'll spend the rest of your life with. We're not talking about things like whether or not the person has money. We're talking about personality and character stuff: Is he funny or great at making conversation? Does she listen well? Is she friendly?

Look for negative qualities also. (That sounds funny, doesn't it?) Like, does she gossip all the time? Or is he constantly boasting about himself? These kinds of traits will be the ones you'll want to avoid.

The point isn't to find someone to marry or even just to date. You're just starting to pay attention to what qualities (good and bad) are important to you.

CHECK OUT GREAT MARRIAGES.

When you see marriages that look fantastic, take notice. What about the relationship seems strong? If you know the couple, or if you're bold, then you can ask the pair to list and describe the things that make their marriage strong.

53. DIVORCE IS NASTY—I WONDER IF IT COULD HAPPEN TO ME

Most relationships—friends, parent-teenager, siblings, boyfriend-girlfriend—experience some conflict from time to time. It's totally normal. But sometimes that conflict gets bigger and super-difficult to unravel—like a knot that gets larger and tighter at the same time.

All kinds of relationships end or change. You're probably not still friends with everyone you were friends with when you were five years old, right? However, marriage is supposed to be a lifelong thing. It's supposed to be a commitment you make to another person that lasts "'til death parts us" (as the bride and groom usually say during their wedding vows). Then again, marriages are just like all other relationships: They always have conflict.

Maybe your parents are divorced; maybe you've seen firsthand how hard a divorce can be on everyone involved. At the very least, you probably have a friend whose parents are divorced. Divorce is usually messy and full of negative stuff like pain, guilt, confusion, and all kinds of other nasty emotions. That's why God doesn't like divorce. God's desire is that marriages are lifelong.

Sometimes divorce is outside the control of one of the spouses. (For example, when one person leaves to pursue a relationship with someone else.) More often, though, divorce happens because of unresolved conflict that's allowed to grow and grow until it seems completely impossible to deal with.

How can you, as a middle schooler, protect yourself from the pain of divorce? We believe there are a few things you can do, even now:

THINK OF MARRIAGE JUST AS GOD THINKS OF MARRIAGE.

God sees marriage as being something permanent, something that's supposed to last a lifetime. If you think a marriage should last only as long as there's no conflict, then you'll be much more likely to get divorced someday. But if you think of marriage—even now—as a relationship in which divorce is *not* an option, then that viewpoint will really help you in the long run.

CHECK OUT STRONG AND HEALTHY MARRIAGES THAT HAVE LASTED A REALLY LONG TIME.

We know we kind of said this in the last chapter. But take notice of couples with great marriages. You might even ask them to tell you what's kept their marriage so strong for so long.

LEARN HOW TO PROCESS CONFLICT WITH PEOPLE YOU CARE ABOUT.

Don't give up on relationships just because you get in a fight or experience some tension. Learning how to work through conflict *now* can have a huge impact on your ability to have a marriage—someday—that will last.

> "MY PARENTS ARE DIVORCED, SO IT KIND OF PUTS ME IN THE MIDDLE. BUT I LIKE MY STEPBROTHER."
>
> —JAKE AND CADE, 7TH GRADE

54. IS IT WEIRD IF I THINK I MAY *NOT* GET MARRIED?

This is one of those chapter titles that's easy to answer in one word: *NO!* But if you want nine words: "Nope, it's not weird at all to think that." (Did you count to make sure there are really nine words? That's the kind of thing we'd do.)

I (Scott) can honestly say that in middle school I *really* doubted whether I'd get married. There was too much fun going on already. What did I need a girlfriend for, much less a wife? (Now I'm married to this way-beautiful woman, and I can't imagine *not* being married. But that's another story.)

Think about it: Just a few years ago, you were out on the playground, running away from the opposite sex. (Or maybe you were running *after* them.) Cooties could be REAL, man! And you sure didn't wanna get 'em.

So as you get older, are you supposed to just wake up one morning and say, "I can't wait to get married!" Nope. Not only that, but *not* getting married is NOT "abnormal."

For some people, not getting married is exactly the right thing. Jesus never married. (We bet there were tons of women who wanted to marry him, though.) Paul—the guy who wrote lots of the books in the New Testament—apparently never got married, either. So if marriage isn't in your future, then you'll be in the company of some great people.

Now here's one of those great news flashes: *You've got time on your side!* Take a deep breath and relax on this one. There's no need to make a decision about marriage today. In fact, it'd be best if you put off making that decision for quite a few years. Too many people get in a hurry to get married. Some people even believe that getting hitched will magically "make them happier." But when Unhappy Single Person gets married, he (or she) almost always turns into Unhappy Married Person. Relying on someone else to make you happy is *not* a good move.

The best thing you can do right now is to keep building your friendships with people of the opposite sex (assuming you've finally figured out that cooties are fictional). That way, if you *do* end up getting married someday, you'll be better prepared as you continue using the stuff you learned from your coed friendships. (Here's a little hint: It's the same stuff that strong marriages are built upon.)

I WAS A MIDDLE SCHOOL DORK!
—MARKO

And now for Marko's moment of unconsciousness. Yes, thanks to my middle school dorkitude, I spent a minute or so completely unconscious, lying flat on my back in an icy parking lot.

It all started with a stupid dork thing that my friend Chris and I thought was funny. Looking back on it now, I have no idea why it was funny; but we sure thought it was funny at the time.

When our church youth group was dismissed, we'd sit on the hoods of the older high school kids' cars so they couldn't leave. That's it. Funny, huh? Well, not so much. But we thought it was a laugh riot. That is, until a high school junior named Dan lost his patience with us.

Dan got tired of our little game one night (which made it that much funnier to us!). He'd pulled his car up near the door of the church (probably to pick up a girlfriend or something) and ran inside. A perfect moment. We plopped ourselves onto his car's hood and waited.

Oh, I should tell you this happened in the middle of winter in Detroit, Michigan; and it was super cold outside. So there Chris and I sat on Dan's hood, all bundled up in our winter coats and snickering.

When Dan came out to his car, he told us to get off. We didn't. We giggled. He told us again, a little more strongly this time. But we still didn't budge. I think—if I remember correctly—we even pretended we couldn't hear him. ("What? Did you say something? We couldn't quite hear you!") Hilarious stuff. No wonder we were so popular (not).

Dan lost it. He got in his car and stepped on the gas—hard. There was ice in the parking lot, but apparently not where Dan's tires were because he actually squealed his tires. And then his car jumped forward.

Chris and me? Well, we rolled up over the top of the car and dropped down onto the pavement behind it—Chris landed on his arm, and I landed on my head. Chris broke his arm; I got a concussion. Smooth move, huh?

That was the last time Chris and I sat on the hood of anyone's car.

RIGHTS AND PRIVILEGES (BARELY LEGAL)

55. DRIVING

It seems pretty crazy that you'll be driving just a few short years from now, huh? We (Marko and Scott) will be sure to stay off the roads around your home when the time comes.

Getting a driver's license is a major teenage "rite of passage" (something that marks the fact that you're growing up and becoming an adult). Ancient tribes might have thrown a party when a girl had her first period, or they may have sent a teenage boy on some kind of a survival quest—all to mark the time when the young person became an adult.

In our world today, it seems like getting a driver's license has become that mark. And most teenagers think of getting a driver's license as a "right": *I deserve to get this license—it's my right—because I am now of the age at which I am allowed to get one.*

Warning: We're going to sound like parents here for a bit (because, um, we are parents). The funny (and sometimes annoying) thing about "rights" is that they *always* come with responsibilities. For instance, it's considered a "right" in our country that all adults—no matter their race, beliefs, gender, or limitations—should be allowed to have employment (a job). But of course, *getting* and *keeping* that job are still the responsibilities of the individual person.

The laws that state when you can get your driver's license and what you can do with it during your first few years of legal driving are decided by the individual states. And these laws are changing a bunch right now. Lots of states are making laws that say a person can get her driver's license when she's 16, but she has to have a parent or another adult in the car whenever she drives during the first year or two. Other states are writing laws that say until you're 18 years old, you can't have more than one other teenager in the car with you when you drive. (This is because research has shown that teenagers tend to make bad driving decisions, especially when there are a bunch of other teenagers riding in the car with them.)

But whatever the limitations, there are still *tons* of responsibilities that come with being able to drive. Think of it this way: You're responsible not only for your own safety (and the safety of the car you're driving), but also the safety of every other person who's driving in a car near you. Whoa. That's a lot of responsibility!

56. VOTING

You've probably learned, in some class at school, about how a democratic government works. And you've probably heard about the importance of voting.

When you turn 18, you'll have the "right" and privilege of voting. This isn't just about choosing a president. There are *all kinds of* things and people to vote for: Senators and congressmen and congresswomen, judges, school board members, as well as new laws and taxes and stuff like that.

We'll be honest with you here: Sometimes exercising your right to vote is really difficult because, in order to make good decisions about how to use your vote, you have to do some studying and some thinking. You have to learn about the candidates and what they believe. You have to learn about the different laws and taxes and about what will happen if they're voted in or not.

This "work" of voting is one of the main reasons why fewer people (especially young adults) vote these days. But if no one votes, then the system doesn't work properly, and we end up with laws and elected officials that no one wants to follow.

Here's the hard truth: If you say you really care about the earth and the environment but you don't vote for elected officials and laws that support those issues, then *you're to blame* when decisions are made at a government level about how to treat the earth. If you don't vote, then you *don't* get to complain. By not voting, you've given up your right to have a voice because you chose not to use your voice (to vote) when you were given the chance.

How does this impact you now, as a middle schooler? In some ways, not at all. Since you don't get to vote yet, it won't really impact you until you're 18. But that doesn't mean you're too young to figure out what it'll be like when you *can* vote. We suggest you do two things:

DECIDE TO BE A VOTER WHEN YOU'RE 18.

Don't buy into the idea that you can't make a difference. Did you know that in the 2000 U.S. presidential election, George W. Bush won the crucial state of Florida by only 537 votes out of 5.8 million cast? If Bush had lost Florida, then he would've lost the election to Al Gore. So don't ever buy into the idea that you can't make a difference.

PAY ATTENTION WHEN ADULTS DECIDE WHAT OR WHOM TO VOTE FOR.

Ask your parents how they decide which candidates to vote for. Ask your teachers. Ask your youth group leaders. Start to learn about the process and in what ways people take the right to vote seriously.

"IT'S NOT THAT BIG A DEAL TO VOTE BECAUSE MY VOTE DOESN'T COUNT MUCH."
—BEN, 6TH GRADE

57. SMOKING AND DRINKING

Sure, we know there are plenty of middle schoolers who smoke and drink. Or at least there are plenty of middle schoolers who smoke and drink once in a while. (Of course, we're talking about drinking alcohol, not milk.)

We also know that all kinds of adults have told you a thousand times before that you shouldn't smoke or drink. But then, we're not stupid. And we know you're not stupid, either. You've probably watched adults smoke and drink before—maybe a few of them are the same adults who told *you* not to smoke and drink. We've also spent enough time with thousands of middle school students to know that your peers often tell you it's cool to do it.

But this chapter isn't about whether or not you make the bad choice to smoke or drink while you're a teenager. This chapter is about what you'll do in the future when it's your "right" to smoke or to drink alcohol. (The legal age, in most states, is 18 for smoking and 21 for drinking alcohol.)

This is a good place to insert a bit of biblical wisdom from that Bible dude named Paul. (He wrote a major chunk of the New Testament.) Here's what Paul has to say:

> "I have the right to do anything," you say—
> but not everything is beneficial.
> "I have the right to do anything"—
> but not everything is constructive.
>
> (1 Corinthians 10:23)

Paul was writing to the church in Corinth about whether or not it was okay to eat certain kinds of meat. Some people said Christians couldn't because the Old Testament law (written for the Jewish people) said so. Other people said those laws didn't apply to Christians.

Paul gives us a super-important wisdom guideline for all kinds of questions like this one. Basically, he's saying that while you might have the "right" to smoke or drink (once you're 18 or 21 years old), that doesn't make it a good choice. Think about it: You also have the "right" to ride your bike at full speed into a brick wall. But it's not beneficial or constructive. (In other words, it's not helpful, and it's not good for you.)

Someday you'll have the "right" to do lots of things, but you still need to use all kinds of wisdom when you're deciding whether to "exercise that right." Smoking and drinking are just two examples.

58. SEX

Yup, this chapter's kinda like chapter 57 (on smoking and drinking). Legally—as far as the U.S. government is concerned—you have the "right" to have sex. But there are some laws about it. For instance, someone who's older than 18 isn't legally allowed to have sex with someone younger than 18. And, of course, you can't legally *force* someone to have sex with you.

But do you remember what Paul wrote to the Corinthians? (Flip back a page and read that verse from 1 Corinthians again.) Just because something is considered legal, that doesn't necessarily make it a good choice. And God has a bunch to say about the subject of sex.

Why do you believe God wants you to wait until you're married to have sex? (No, seriously, think about that for a minute.) What's your answer? Is it because God is old-fashioned? Is it because God thinks sex is nasty? Neither is true. God *invented* sex. God thinks sex is great! And God wants us to experience it and enjoy it—in the way God designed it (as married people, of course).

God gives us guidelines about sex because God loves us so much. Really! God knows you can seriously mess up your life (in so many ways) by using sex in a way other than how he intended it. And God doesn't want you to mess up your life.

So, just like with so many other things in life, as an adult you'll have the "right" to have sex. You'll have the right to use a chainsaw, to swim with sharks, to give a speech on a street corner, and to say what you really believe—about anything. You'll also have the right to become an airline pilot or a trash collector, a gunmaker or an art dealer. *All of those things* are good and helpful (some even beautiful or fun) when done in the right time, right place, and right context. Yet all of those things could become ugly, messy, destructive, boring, or uncomfortable if done in the wrong time, wrong place, or wrong way.

Make sense?

59. TAXES (HUH?)

Wow. It's a little weird to have a chapter about taxes follow chapters on smoking and drinking and sex. But remember, this section of the book is all about the rights and privileges that will come in your future.

Wait. Are taxes a "right" or a "privilege"?

Well, that's a fine question. *No one* likes to pay taxes. No one fills out those income tax forms and thinks, *This is awesome! I get to give more money to the government! Yippee! I wonder if I could give them even MORE?*

So why did we (Marko and Scott, nutjobs that we are) include this chapter in our book? Well, because taxes are in your future, oh wonderful middle school friend. Plus, taxes are just a part of the privilege of living in a free, democratic country. And they also help pay for some of your rights.

Here are a few things you'll be glad to pay taxes for someday:

- Police (You may not be glad when one gives you a speeding ticket, but you'll certainly be grateful when a police officer helps you or your friend.)

- Firefighters (You may not be thrilled when you have to pull your car over so they can speed past you, but you'll appreciate them if your house is ever on fire.)

- Teachers (Okay, you may not be thankful for your math teacher, but one day you'll certainly be glad you had teachers.)

- Road signs and roads

- Help for people who've experienced a major crisis (like a flood or fire)

- National forests (to visit and to keep some oxygen pumping back into the air)

- Jails and prisons (to keep criminals from hurting you)

- Politicians (to help us stay on friendly terms with other countries)

- And so much more!

Our tax dollars pay for all of these things, and they're all privileges. One day you'll have a right to them, too. (You kinda have a right to them now; but it'll be different when you're the one paying the taxes.)

Paying taxes might not seem like much of a right or a privilege. Fair enough. We (Marko and Scott) pay taxes, so we know it's not fun to do. But we also know that paying them provides for many of the rights and privileges that we sure wouldn't want to give up.

DEATH

60. WHAT TO DO WITH THE SADNESS

Before we get to the topic of this chapter (dealing with our sadness when someone dies), let's start with the subject of death.

There's a common expression: "In this world nothing is certain but death and taxes." (Benjamin Franklin said it first.) We already talked about taxes in chapter 59, so now we're ready to discuss death.

Of course you know that everyone dies. But there were two guys in the Old Testament (Elijah and Enoch) who didn't. Both Elijah and Enoch were actually taken up to heaven without experiencing death first. (You can read about them in Genesis 5 and 2 Kings 2.) We (Marko and Scott) think going straight to heaven would be way cool, but we're not spending much time hoping for it to happen to us since, well, it happened to just those two guys.

So isn't it interesting that we all get sad about something that happens to everyone? (Really, it happens to every living thing.) It's totally natural to feel sad about death. Death feels massively final. And if the person who dies is someone you care about, then you know that relationship is over in some way.

It's even pretty normal to feel sad about the death of someone you don't know. Maybe you've heard about the death of someone in your community or even someone on the other side of the world. Stories like this make us sad because we know other people are in pain. They've lost someone close to them, and we feel sad because we know they're sad.

So what do we do with our sadness when someone dies? We (Marko and Scott) have some "what not to do" advice, as well as some "what to do" advice for you.

Our "what not to do" advice is this: Don't stuff your sadness somewhere deep inside you. Don't hide it away. Don't pretend you're not sad. That's unhealthy and bad for you in SO many ways (physically, emotionally, spiritually, mentally, relationally).

On the other hand, our "what to do" advice is just the opposite: Talk about it. *Talk about it* with your parents, your friends, your youth group leaders. And talk about it with God. Seriously. God would love to help you with your sadness. That doesn't mean God will just take it away, but God wants to be with you in the middle of your sadness.

61. LIFE ISN'T FAIR: PAIN AND SUFFERING

This is a tough one. We wish we had a nice and neat answer for you, like:

> *Life only seems unfair because you're not grown up yet.*
>
> *Disease and pain exist because you sin.*
>
> *Everything is better if you stop and smell the flowers.*

Or some other completely ridiculous, untrue explanation. But we're committed to being honest with you. So we'll be honest now: Disease and pain and stuff like that are a major, major bummer, and we don't completely understand them.

I mean, sure, we could give you the "right" answers: Pain (and evil in general) exists in the world because God created us with the freedom to choose. If we were robots who were capable of choosing to do only good, then there wouldn't be any pain. But it's better for us (and for God) that we have the freedom to choose. And some pain happens because of our choices; some pain happens because of other people's choices. That all makes sense to us.

The tougher thing to explain is the pain and suffering that has nothing to do with someone's choice.

Let's start with this, though: A *lot* of pain and suffering that doesn't appear—at first glance—to be the result of someone's choice actually is. Like, when you see pictures of children starving in other countries. Well, we could fix that problem pretty easily. There's plenty of food in the world. And plenty of money. But people (and companies and countries) with more resources than they need may choose to keep it all for themselves. That's an evil choice, and it results in those children starving to death.

What's really tough to understand is an event like a tsunami or an earthquake that kills thousands of people. No human played a role in that. And many really smart people have written lots of books about the subject (which are really hard to read). But those books don't agree with each other, either.

What we can tell you is this: God doesn't often step in and redirect things like hurricanes and tsunamis. Nor does God "cause" them to happen. But that doesn't mean God isn't interested or aware of what's going on here on earth. God is *with us*—right in the middle of all our pain, suffering, questions, and complaints.

"WE CRY WHEN WE GET SHOTS BECAUSE IT HURTS. PEOPLE IN AFRICA CRY FROM HAPPINESS WHEN THEY GET A SHOT BECAUSE THEY KNOW IT HELPS THEM."

—ASHLIE, 8TH GRADE

62. HARPS AND CLOUDS—WHAT'S HEAVEN *REALLY* LIKE?

We gotta be honest with you: This is a tough one. Some people claim they've "seen" heaven, but that's pretty hard to believe. Still, almost everyone has wondered at one time or another—*What's heaven really like?*

It seems like every cartoon illustrates it the same way: People dressed in long white robes with wings on their backs, slowly strolling around from cloud to cloud, strumming on harps. (Who made the harp the official instrument of heaven, anyway? Why not an electric guitar? Or a kazoo?) Are we the only ones who don't get fired up about listening to soft harp music for the rest of eternity?

If that picture doesn't thrill you, either, then you're in luck. That's NOT the picture of heaven the Bible paints.

In John 14:2, Jesus says, "My Father's house has plenty of room; if that were not so, would I have told you that I am going there to prepare a place for you?" The Bible uses words like *rooms*, and *house*, and *place* because heaven is a very real location. God wants us to understand, so God gives us familiar images. God also wants us to know that there's a personalized location waiting for us.

Revelation 21 says heaven is a place of "no more death or mourning or crying or pain" (v. 4). There's no sadness in heaven—picture that! No funerals, no getting grounded, no hatred, no wars, no racism, no divorce, no homework, no vegetables (we can hope!), and no one feels left out. Heaven is where we'll live with God and worship God forever.

But before you start thinking that "worship God forever" really means "a super-boring never-ending sing-along," remember that *worship* means more than just music. Worship involves responding to God with all that you do. And since there's no sadness in heaven, then that means there can't be boredom, right? So there must be plenty of cool stuff for us to do!

Keep in mind that you can't *earn* your way to heaven. Being right with God—and ending up in heaven—all starts by realizing your own sins and shortcomings. Then you must recognize that when Jesus died on the cross—after living a perfect life—he paid for your sins and mine. And finally, it all depends on you inviting Jesus to be the Leader of your life. Have you ever done that? If so, then not only do you have heaven to look forward to, but you also have God's perfect love to guide you through *this* life.

"HOW DO WE KNOW WHAT WE HAVE TO DO EACH DAY
TO BE GOOD ENOUGH TO GET INTO HEAVEN?"
—HANNAH, 7TH GRADE

63. I DON'T WANT TO DIE

At some point in your life, you look around and realize that *every* person was once a little baby. Crazy thought, isn't it? Can you imagine your grandma or grandpa as a little diaper-filling, thumb-sucking, drooling toddler?

Then, at the other end of life, you look around and realize that at some point everyone's going to die. So far, there's not been one person in recorded history who didn't die. Well, that's not completely true. The Bible says there were two people who didn't actually die. Enoch "walked faithfully with God; then he was no more, because God took him away" (Genesis 5:24). And Elijah was taken up to heaven in a whirlwind (2 Kings 2). Pretty slick. But everyone else has died.

First off—lots of people are scared to die because they don't know what'll happen to them afterward. That could be pretty scary to think about. But if you really do know Jesus and if you've invited him to lead your life and walk with you every day, then Jesus will keep on walking with you all the way to heaven. And heaven, as we talked about in chapter 62, is a pretty amazing place. From what we can tell, once you get there—you're never gonna want to leave!

This is how Paul put it in Philippians 1:21 (CEV): "If I live, it will be for Christ, and if I die, I will gain even more." That's a pretty great way to view death.

But before we get too carried away with all this talk about death, we should mention that it makes total sense that you don't want to die. See, God put you on this planet for a reason. A whole lot of reasons, actually. God has a mission for you. God wants you to live and to laugh and, most importantly, to *love people.*

Your life really does have a purpose. It's to love God with all of your heart and to love people. People are God's greatest treasure. Think about this: You'll never look into the eyes of someone who God isn't crazy about. And while you're living out your one and only life, God wants you to love those people, too.

You probably know some people who don't know about God's gigantic love for them. *You* can play a key role in helping them understand. *If* you take a risk, that is. *You* can care for people who are hurting. You can help people who are sick or in need or "on the outside." You can help them understand that death is not the end.

Maybe the reason you don't want to die is because God has so much LIFE yet for you to live. Everyone gets one life. It's up to you—and only you—to make the most of yours.

"WHEN YOU WERE BORN, YOU WERE CRYING. MAKE YOUR LIFE WORTHWHILE SO THAT WHEN YOU DIE YOU'RE SMILING!

—ASHLIE, 8TH GRADE

FOR YOUR GENERATION

64. GLOBAL WARMING

Man, it's getting hot in here! (Ha! We're so funny, we make ourselves laugh!)

No, seriously. By now we're sure you've heard about the problem of global warming. There are a few holdouts here and there who are still denying that it's happening. But science and weather peeps seem to have won the argument already. And the facts speak for themselves: Glaciers are disappearing (shockingly fast, when you think of how long they've been there); average temperatures are rising (bit by bit, but each bit makes a massive difference); extreme weather—hurricanes and all kinds of weather stuff—that used to occur only once in a while is now regular ol' news.

If things keep changing the way they have been, then we're going to be in some serious trouble 20 years from now. We also have a pretty good idea that all of this is happening because of us silly humans and all the junk we pump into the atmosphere.

But hold on: This isn't a book about the environment. This is a book about you and God and your future. And since Christians seem to have very different ideas about how we should respond to global warming, it seems like a good idea to think about God's perspective.

Some questions: *What do you suppose God thinks about the earth (not just the planet, but everything on it)? Do you think God hates the earth and just wants it to get toasted—after pulling believers out at the last moment? Or do you think God loves the earth—not just people, but the whole planet and everything in it?*

We believe (pretty strongly, really) that God totally loves his creation. C'mon—God invented it! Just look at the first chapter of Genesis and all those "God said it was good" phrases at the end of each creation day. Just because there's sin in the world doesn't mean God wants to chuck this beautiful creation into the trash.

So what can you do about it? Sure, we need some big answers—solutions from big companies and governments and stuff. But we also need millions of little answers. And one of those little answers—one of those little solutions—is YOU. As you grow up, you'll have more chances either to *add* to this problem or *help* this problem. Do you love God's creation like God does?

65. WAR

War really stinks, doesn't it? But the tough reality is that as long as people are on earth, and as long as people continue to have differences (which seems pretty normal), there will be wars.

Really, there's almost never been a time when war didn't exist. If you read through parts of the Old Testament, you'll see that war was a regular part of life.

Of course, people's lives get ruined in wars—and not just "the bad people." There are always innocent people who get hurt as well.

Christians have a bunch of different opinions about war. And they all feel pretty strongly that they can back up their arguments with the Bible. There are extreme opinions on both sides, of course. Like, Christians should *never* support or be a part of a war because Jesus came to bring peace and said we should "turn the other cheek." Or, on the other end, Christians should use whatever methods they need to use, including war, to protect their way of life. And lots of people believe something in the middle: War isn't good and should be avoided, but it's sometimes necessary—especially to combat evil.

We (Marko and Scott) aren't going to take a strong position on war in this book because it's something you need to work out with your family, your church, and your own study of the Bible.

But we'll "hint" a bit and say that it doesn't seem like we should take our direction from the wars of the Old Testament as much as we should take our direction from Jesus.

Why is this chapter in this book? Because—as a follower of Jesus—you're going to have to decide what you think about war. You might have an opinion now, and that's great. But when you're older, you'll have a real opportunity and responsibility to influence this issue. You'll do this mainly by voting, but you'll also have the chance to influence others' decisions and actions by how you talk about war and the other actions you take.

You can't hide from the issue of war (not unless you stick your head in the sand like some kind of scared ostrich). So start asking questions. Ask adults why they believe what they do about war. And talk to people who have different opinions about it.

"WHY FIGHT IF NO ONE REALLY WINS?"
—JAMES, 7TH GRADE

66. AIDS

By now, everyone's heard of HIV (human immuno-deficiency virus) and AIDS (acquired immune deficiency syndrome) and the millions of lives that have been lost to this disease. Let's start with a few basics, though, just to make sure you know what it is.

HIV is a virus, which means it's in the blood, and it can't be passed through the air like bacteria. It messes up certain cells in a person's body—mostly cells that help fight off other infections. AIDS is what happens when HIV isn't treated. It makes it so the body can't fight off all sorts of diseases. People don't actually die *from* HIV or AIDS—they die from other infections or diseases.

Since HIV is a disease that's carried in the blood, it's passed from one person to another through anything that causes their blood to be in contact. Sex is the most common way, but other blood contact or contact with other body fluids (like a mother who breastfeeds her child, or two drug users who share the same needle) can also spread the disease.

So why is there a chapter about AIDS in a book about your future?

Well, the AIDS crisis in America is mostly under control these days. People are more cautious than they were 20 years ago. And now there are medicines to help those with HIV manage their symptoms. People still die of AIDS in the United States, but it's not as "for sure" as it was even 10 years ago.

So the reason we included this chapter is because there's still a massive AIDS crisis all over the world—especially in Africa. Millions of people (moms, dads, children) are infected with HIV/AIDS, and millions have already died. The tough thing is that we *have* medicine to help these people, but we're not very good at getting it to them.

Our generation (Marko and Scott's) hasn't done a very good job of figuring out how to really help people. Our generation has been selfish, or perhaps we've spent more time passing the blame than finding a solution. ("It's your own fault you have AIDS"—which is sometimes true and sometimes not.) We need your generation to solve this crisis.

We don't throw around "What would Jesus do?" very often (if ever). But this issue offers a perfect example of a time when we need to ask that question. Would Jesus sit back and blame people? Would Jesus sit back and wait for someone else to do something? We don't think so.

> "I THINK AIDS IS A HUGE PROBLEM, BUT PEOPLE DON'T HAVE THE GUTS TO DO ANYTHING ABOUT IT."
>
> —NATALIE, 8TH GRADE

67. GAS PRICES, ENERGY CRISES, AND AN OUT-OF-CONTROL PLANET

This chapter is 100 percent connected to the one about global warming. So if you haven't read that one yet, take a minute to go back and read chapter 64 first.

We (Marko and Scott) remember the days—not all that long ago—when gasoline cost less than $1 per gallon. As we write this, gas prices have been hovering around $3 a gallon. It's crazy to think about what the prices could be by the time you read this. Or even crazier—by the time you're buying your own gas!

There are two main problems fueling energy, oil, and gas problems (Ha! Fueling! Get it?): These two problems are 1) people and, 2) people.

The first people-problem has to do with the number of people living on earth, and, even more, the number of people using energy resources like gas and oil. There are a lot of people in the world, and while humans seem to be pretty good at having more babies, we're not so good at thinking ahead to make sure we have enough resources (the stuff in this chapter, plus stuff like food) for everyone.

The second people-problem is greed. You know what greed is, right? It's that selfish desire to take care of only you and ignore everyone else. Greed is part of the energy problem because companies and individuals (like you and like us) make decisions that can hurt our world—because we're thinking only of ourselves.

If humans are going to be around in the future, then we're going to have to make some big-time changes! Your generation has to figure out this stuff. Our generation is finally starting to get serious about it; but you guys will inherit a bunch of the problems we helped create. (Sorry 'bout that!)

A HUGE part of this issue surrounds oil. We have to figure out ways not to use so much of it. Not only is it getting more expensive, but we're also learning more all the time about how much the use of oil (in gasoline and other things) hurts the planet.

Do you want to make a huge difference in the world? If your generation can make some progress in this area, it will bring great change to our planet—God's creation.

68. ROBOTS AND FLYING CARS? STUFF WE CAN'T PICTURE RIGHT NOW

First, we have to say it seems really weird to go from chapters about the AIDS crisis and energy problems (if you're reading these chapters in order) to a chapter about robots and flying cars. Not quite the same thing, huh? But, hey, this is a book about you and your future. And this particular section of the book is designed to respond to the questions we hear from middle schoolers about their generation's future.

Let's talk change for a minute. Check this out:

- It took 38 years for radio to reach an audience of 50 million people. It took 13 years for TV to reach that many viewers. It took only four years for the Internet to reach that many users.

- The first text message was sent in 1992. Today, more text messages are sent *every day* than there are people on earth.

- More than 2.7 *billion* searches are performed on Google every month.

- There are more than five times as many words in the English language as there were in Shakespeare's time (1600).

- In 10 years there will be more English speakers in China than in any other country on earth.

- The amount of new techincal information in the world is doubling every two years. By the year 2010, it's expected to double every 72 hours.

Crazy, huh? Especially considering the fact that when we (Marko and Scott) were your age, these things didn't even exist:

- Cell phones

- Cable TV

- CDs and DVDs

- Hand-held gaming systems

- Personal computers of any kind (desktop or laptop)

- Fax machines (which are sooooo old school now!)

- The Internet

- And a whole lot more

So, will your generation live on the moon? Wow! Who knows? Anything seems possible. And everything seems unpredictable. It's difficult to guess the future from more than a couple of years away. So instead of trying to figure out the future of technology and how it will impact our lives, it's probably better to think about change and how that impacts our lives right now.

Are you ready for change?

IMAGINE

69. ARE YOU A DREAMER? DREAMING BIG DREAMS

Ever get in a fight with your brother or sister?

Maybe you remember the story of Joseph from Genesis 37. (Check it out—you'll like it.) He was one of *12* brothers, and Joseph had big dreams about what God might do with his life. Joseph loved God, he followed God, and God told Joseph he had big plans for Joseph's life. But Joseph's brothers "hated him" for it. (Their hatred might have had something to do with how often Joseph told them that God had big plans for him; boasting isn't usually such a great idea.)

One day when Joseph was about 17 years old (not much older than you), his brothers were out taking care of their father's flocks. Joseph's dad sent him out to the fields to see how his brothers were doing. When they saw their younger brother coming, they said to one another, "Here comes that dreamer!" (verse 19) They started to talk about *killing* Joseph. Now that's some serious sibling rivalry.

Think about the words they used: "Here comes that dreamer!" Do you think they meant it as a compliment? No chance! They might as well have said, "Here comes that PUNK little brother of ours!" Fantasy-boy. Delusion-dork.

But in God's ears, *dreamer* is the ultimate compliment.

Don't let anyone convince you that you're too young to make a difference in your school, community, or even in the world. But be ready—cuz they'll try. Even if they don't say it out loud, sometimes you'll get the feeling that people are thinking, *He's too immature.* Or *She's not ready yet.* And sometimes those dream-killers can discourage you to the point where you actually believe you're "too young."

We beg you—DON'T LET THAT HAPPEN!

Here's a verse that everyone younger than 20 should memorize. Paul said to Timothy: "Don't let anyone look down on you because you are young, but set an example for the believers in speech, in conduct, in love, in faith and in purity" (1 Timothy 4:12).

Where does God need *you* to be a dreamer and set an example for people? Is there a situation that makes you think, *That's just not right!* but you're not sure you can make a difference?

Before you read the next sentence, ask God, *What do you want me to dream about?* (Did you ask? Good!) Then start asking God on a regular basis to help you be the dreamer God made you to be.

70. FEAR: THE ENEMY OF IMAGINATION

This chapter's not about the kind of fear you might think of first. Not the fear you'd feel if you were looking into the jaws of a gigantic alligator. Not the kind of fear you'd feel if you stayed out all night and had to face your parents' anger. We're talking about the fear of "being different."

A crazy thing happens when we get to middle school. You've experienced it. So have we. It's the need to fit in. Now sometimes that's good—it helps us live with each other. It's what keeps you from going to school in your swimsuit, or sneezing into your classmate's face, or screaming in a library.

But the need to fit in—and the fear of *not* fitting in—is an imagination killer. It can sink your hopes and dreams.

In kindergarten *everybody* has a great imagination, don't they? (Think back to all of your Crayola creations.) But over the next few years, kids start to listen to other people's comments—and criticisms. "Why did you color that tree purple? Trees aren't purple." "Your lines aren't straight." "You call *that* art?" And before long, the fear of not fitting in—of caring too much about others' opinions—becomes more important than imagination.

That's garbage!

When we're afraid to RISK, we bail out on the things that God wants to bring into the world through us. Peer pressure, insecurity—call it whatever you want, but God made you to be an original. Middle school can trap you into chasing what other people *want* you to be, instead of the one and only whom God *made* you to be.

The Bible says God didn't give you a spirit of fear but a spirit of boldness (Romans 8:15). Are you willing to do things a little differently as you grow into the YOU that God intended you to become?

Little by little, we need to overcome the fear that freezes us up. **What are you *not* doing because you're afraid?** Is there a hobby or sport or club you want to try? Is there a friend you want to talk to about God? Is there a conversation you want to have?

Make *today* the day you take a swing at that fear!

> For I am the Lord, your God
> who takes hold of your right hand and says to you,
> **Do not fear**; I will help you.
>
> (Isaiah 41:13, emphasis added)

"WHAT MIGHT HAPPEN IN THE FUTURE CAN BE SCARY [TO THINK ABOUT], BUT YOU HAVE TO FOCUS ON TODAY."

—DANTE, 7TH GRADE

71. PAYING ATTENTION TO YOUR PASSIONS

Passion. Enthusiasm. Excitement. Interest. Zest.

These words all mean close to the same thing. But another way to put it is to ask, "What do you get *fired up* about?"

Have you ever heard of passion fruit? Just so you know, the "passion" we're talking about here is different than that kind. (It's not as fruity.) It's not the smoochy-romance kind of passion, either. (Sorry, there are no making-out stories anywhere on this page.)

Okay, back to our topic—passion!

There are some middle school girls I know who are fired up about helping single moms. It kinda got started when they found out a single mom with disabilities could really use some help. She lived near them, so they decided to do some yard work for her. They bought and planted some flowers in her yard—and they also formed a bond with her. Now these girls are collecting change (by putting canisters in some local businesses) for another single mom who needs a new starter in her car. Guess you could say they have a growing "passion" for single moms. And they're making a difference.

I know some junior high guys who're fired up about helping elementary school students. Nearly every week, they make the Bible come to life for younger kids at our church. Sometimes they get a little kid's runny-nose juice on their shirts, but they know they're making a difference.

What's YOUR passion?

Ask yourself, *Where could I get excited about seeing a difference being made? What comes to your mind?*

See, God puts passions in people's hearts so that people will act and impact the world. So when you feel something really pulling on your heart, it could be because God is trying to energize that passion inside you. Specific needs can fire up your passion—like orphaned kids or hungry people. Specific areas can also fire you up, like a passion for music or computers.

God has a passion, too. It's *people*. That's why Jesus was willing to die for us—we are his passion. And Jesus wants our passions to ultimately point people toward him.

That's way better than the best-tasting passion fruit on any tree.

72. CHURCH

Think about your church—how would you describe it? Good, bad, or somewhere in-between?

Here's a question for a dreamer to answer: No matter how you described your church, how can *you* make it even better?

In chapter 47 of this book, we talked about how the church is really made up of people. YOU are one of those people.

Dreamers realize they're not too young to be a part of what God's doing.

In my house I'm (Scott) in charge of putting the recycling bin at the end of the driveway on trash day. But some weeks I have to do it kind of sneakily. See, one of my sons has a great imagination, and almost every week he sees me throwing away stuff that I see as trash but he sees as "possibility." He always uses the same phrase: "Hey, I could DO something with that!" Then he takes the item and invents his own game or weapon or solar-powered, life-sized motorcycle. (Okay, he hasn't made that last one yet, but he might do it soon.)

Do you know what God says when he sees you?

"I could DO something with that!"

Think about these questions and dream a little:

- How's the *youth ministry* at your church? What might God want to do *through you* to make it even better?

- How does your church *welcome* new people? What might God want to do *through you* to make it even better?

- How does your church care for *little kids?* What might God want to do *through you* to make it even better?

- What's an area you're passionate about? (Check out chapter 71 if you don't know what *passion* is.) What might God want to do *through you* to impact your church with that passion?

Maybe you're getting the feeling that a church is only as strong as the commitment of the people who go there. So true!

Don't let your gifts and skills and passions get taken to the curb and thrown away with the trash. Let God take those things and DO something with them to make his church an even better place. You won't believe how good it makes you feel.

73. END OF POVERTY

You wanna dream big? Okay. How 'bout the topic of this chapter?

Poverty basically means having little or no money or material possessions. Not the kind of "no money" that means "not enough cash to go to the movies." More like you don't have enough food. No medicine. You have only the clothes on your back and shelter that doesn't protect you from the weather.

Sound severe? Unfortunately, it is.

More than eight million people around the world die each year because they're too poor to survive. Sometimes those kinds of numbers can be hard to grasp. So think of it this way: A large basketball arena (say, the Chicago Bulls' stadium) seats about 20,000 people. That's how many people will die *tomorrow* because of poverty. Gulp.

Now, some people might *really* call you a *crazy* dreamer if you told them that your dream is to see the *end* of poverty. But our question is—WHY NOT?

We're *not* saying this is a simple, easy dream. If it were, then someone would've figured it out by now. But it IS a worthwhile, God-given dream. Imagine if one of the people at risk of dying tomorrow wasn't just some unknown face on the other side of the world. Imagine it's your mom. Or your little brother. Or your best friend. Or...you. All of a sudden it'd be a pretty big deal, right?

Here's the thing. Most of us don't worry about how we'll get our next meal, or where we'll sleep tonight, or having clothes to keep us warm and dry. We didn't do anything to be born into a family that has enough. It just—happened. But Luke 12:48 says,

> From everyone who has been given much,
> much will be demanded;
> and from the one who has been entrusted with
> much, much more will be asked.

In 2008, the United States will spend more than $600 billion (that's $600,000,000,000) on military costs. But it spends less than one-thirtieth as much on helping the poorest of the poor. Sorry to throw a bunch of numbers at you...that's not the point. The point is the state of our *hearts*. Smart people who study poverty say this generation could end extreme poverty by 2025! But that'll never happen without some dreaming. Without people's hearts changing—one at a time—so a stadium full of people don't have to die needlessly every day. What about you? What about your heart?

God is dreaming about the end of poverty. Let's dream with God. And if that dreaming leads to action, then poverty really can be beaten.

74. CAN MY GENERATION REALLY MAKE THE WORLD A BETTER PLACE?

That's a HUGE question, huh? Well, we (Marko and Scott) are committed to telling you the straight truth, and the answer to "Can my generation really make the world a better place?" is...

No.

Ah, we're only kidding. OF COURSE! *Big time! Yes! For sure! Totally! Unquestionably! Absolutely!* (We could go on for a *long time* giving you more words that mean "yes," but you'd get bored.)

Let's back up a step: YOU can make the world a better place. Seriously. And here's the super-cool thing: God wants to partner with you in making the world a better place. God is inviting you to bring about change—good change.

We're not talking about some day in the future (even though that's what this book is about). We're talking about you changing the world NOW. We have a 15-year-old friend who started an organization to end modern-day slavery. He's already raised hundreds of thousands of dollars that have been used to free hundreds of slaves. And we know dozens (even hundreds) of kids your age who change the world every single day in ways that people may not notice as much.

When you and your friends get together to make a difference and God gives the whole thing a bit o' power—watch out!

So this truth reveals another question: What does it mean to "make the world a better place"? Start with creation—the beginning of "the story" as we know it. What does God want for his creation? Things like beauty, creativity, and purity. Now move forward through the Bible and discover what else God values: Justice (helping those who are being taken advantage of), mercy (showing compassion to people), love (uh, you know, not hate).

Jesus sums it up this way: "Love the Lord your God with all your heart and with all your soul and with all your mind," and "Love your neighbor as yourself" (Matthew 22:37, 39). Dude! Seriously, if you live that out, you will rock the world!

A FINAL THOUGHT

75. *YOUR* AMAZING FUTURE

There are three more cool things we want to share with you about the future.

Really, really, really cool. Really. And Cool.

First is this...

THE FUTURE IS HAPPENING—RIGHT NOW!

Did you feel it? You just stepped into it. (Well, you didn't actually *step* cuz you're probably sitting down as you read this book, unless you're walking while you're reading. And that's a whole other issue.) But you're IN it—you're in the future! And now—just a second later—it's the past.

Part of the future is the Distant Future. You know, the time when we'll all have cell-phone-TV-Internet gadgets built into the palms of our hands, and we'll be able to travel in ways that haven't even been thought up yet.

But the Near Future is just about to happen. Here...it...comes!

BUT THE SECOND THING, AND PROBABLY THE VERY COOLEST, IS THIS: YOU HAVE AN INCREAS-ING AMOUNT OF INFLUENCE ON WHAT YOUR OWN FUTURE WILL LOOK LIKE.

Think about it—when you were a little kid, you couldn't control much of your future at all. Somebody decided what food you ate, what clothes you wore, who you hung out with. About the only thing you got to decide was when to fill your diaper.

But as you get older, your future is more and more and more about *your* decisions. It's more and more in *your* control. You have a say in it. It really is Your Future!

Who will your friends be? That's your choice. What will you spend your time doing? How much time will you spend having crazy fun? How much time will you spend learning? How much time will you spend helping people? Where will God fit into the mix? Those are all your decisions to make. And those decisions will shape your future. No pressure... (Yeah, right.)

Just think: In a little more than four years, you'll be done with high school. And at that point you'll be really close to being 100 percent in charge of how you'll design your future. But the stuff you're deciding right now is also shaping your Distant Future—and the future you're stepping into—now!

AND FINALLY, REMEMBER YOU DON'T HAVE TO DO IT ALONE!
Jesus is honestly right there with you. He's ready to live the great times with you and help you handle the junk. So be sure you invite him along—and dive into *your* amazing future.

Life and faith can be hard when you're in middle school. But this book gives you all the tips and secrets you need to really grasp your faith and keep hold of it. *My Faith* is filled with quick and easy-to-read topics along with funny stories from the authors. Plus there are quotes and questions from students just like you.

My Faith
Kurt Johnston and Mark Oestreicher
RETAIL $9.99
ISBN 978-0-310-27382-0

When you're in middle school, everything is changing—your body, your emotions, your school, and maybe even your friends are different. Now your parents and siblings are trying to figure out why you're different, and you wish they could understand you! This book will give you secrets and tips that will show you how you can help to make your family even better.

My Family
Kurt Johnston and Mark Oestreicher
RETAIL $9.99
ISBN 978-0-310-27430-8

Your friends are some of the most important people in your life. Make sure you know everything that makes friendships work, and what not to do in a friendship. This book will show you how to make friends, how to be a great friend, and insider tips to everything else you need to know about keeping those friendships.

My Friends
Kurt Johnston and Mark Oestreicher
RETAIL $9.99
ISBN 978-0-310-27881-8

Visit www.invertbooks.com or your local bookstore.

KURT JOHNSTON
MARK OESTREICHER

::MYSCHOOL

MS+SCH
MIDDLE SCHOOL SURVIVAL SERIES

Middle school can feel overwhelming at times, with so many things that are new and different. From pop quizzes to changing clothes for gym class, there are plenty of new (and sometimes scary) experiences! But don't worry—this book will give you all the tips you need to survive and thrive in middle school, in a fun and easy-to-read format.

My School
Kurt Johnston and Mark Oestreicher
RETAIL $9.99
ISBN 978-0-310-27882-5

There never seems to be enough time or money. Find the wisdom you need to help you use these resources to better your life and the world around you. As you explore the motivations behind how you use your time and money, the practical tips and biblical insights in this book will show you how you can manage these resources better.

Wisdom On...Time & Money
Mark Matlock
RETAIL $9.99
ISBN 978-0-310-27928-0

We all love a good song, movie, or TV show. But not everything out there is good for us. This book won't tell you what you should not listen to or watch. Instead this book is filled with principles to help you gain the wisdom needed to help you make wise choices about what you choose to be entertained by.

Wisdom On...Music, Movies & Television
Mark Matlock
RETAIL $9.99
ISBN 978-0-310-27931-0

If you've ever felt lonely, abandoned, lost, or unloved, you're not alone. Although she's a successful Gotee recording artist today, Stephanie Smith has had her fair share of hurt and heartbreak. Growing up fatherless, she struggled with her identity, self-esteem, and so much more. But today she's found hope in God that she believes can help you through your own heartaches and brokenness.

Crossroads
The Teenage Girl's Guide to Emotional Wounds
Stephanie Smith
RETAIL $9.99
ISBN 978-0-310-28550-2

After bizarre events at their New York concert, P.O.D. must decipher mysterious visions and battle evil forces to locate "The Chosen." Armed with super powers, Sunny, Wuv, Traa, and Marcos must fight alien Xenophon warriors and prevent the mysterious being, known only as The Soul Shredder, from getting to The Chosen first. Saving the world was never so tough—or so crucial!

P.O.D. The Nexus
Matt Broome
RETAIL $14.99
ISBN 978-0-310-71638-9

Visit www.invertbooks.com or your local bookstore.

Suddenly, it seems like everything in your life is changing.
Your friends expect way too much from you. You fight with
your parents more than you'd like. You just don't understand
why your life seems so chaotic now. You are not alone. If
you're feeling overwhelmed or confused with your life, this
book will help you understand who you are, and give you hope
for who you're becoming.

Mirrors & Maps
A Girl's Guide to Becoming a Teen
Melissa Trevathan and Sissy Goff
RETAIL $16.99
ISBN 978-0-310-27918-1

Visit www.invertbooks.com or your local bookstore.

Students today are bombarded with opinions and research about Jesus that go against everything you've been trying to teach them. They don't know if they can trust what the Bible says about Jesus because they don't know they can trust the Bible. They wonder if he really rose from the dead, or if he was even God. Let Lee Strobel's investigations into the real Jesus help your students see the truth about the Son of God.

The Case for the Real Jesus—Student Edition
A Journalist Investigates Current Challenges to Christianity
Lee Strobel with Jane Vogel
RETAIL $9.99
ISBN 978-0-310-28323-2